This book delivers a step-by  o-
how you identify yourself, your external roles, your
possessions, and your unconscious negative assumptions.

The book helps you re-identify with your True Self and
become free from:

- the fear of being unacceptable
- feeling unworthy
- the fear of not being enough
- second-guessing yourself

And the power to:

- be the person you know you can be
- have greater self-acceptance,
  self-appreciation and self-love
- break through what has been holding you
  back personally

By applying a Self-Discovery System for living a life of
authenticity, you will experience more:

- — Confidence in yourself
- — Determination to pursue your purpose
- — Energy and improved health
- — Close relationships with yourself and others
- — Courage to live your passion

"The way Jack has personally pulled his experience into the book is very powerful for people who are struggling with trying to make the next transition, but are being held back from past mental models, and lack of understanding who they are outside of the business. I have read many self-help books, and do not know of any that 'cut to the heart of the issue' as this book has. It is practical and insightful, and the worksheets at the end of the chapters really help drive the concept."

-Dave Sinclair, Edmonton, Canada

"*7 Principles for Living with Authenticity* is the ideal guidebook for anyone who feels there may be more to life and who is looking for a structured, easy to follow approach to guide their personal exploration. It comes at a time where ever increasing numbers of us grapple with transitions - from full-time work or business to the next phase of their lives, empty nesters, career transitions and so on – when our old identity is called into question and we re-evaluate what really matters in life. Jack has applied lessons learned from his own life experiences in finding his true self to create a unique and practical self-help process. His seven principles to leading an authentic life are explained by reference to the latest scientific discoveries and everyday examples, thus enabling the reader to easily understand and identify with them. Jack's simple yet effective exercises provide a roadmap for the path to self-discovery – once the realm of esoteric teachings, but now readily accessible to all. Put simply, in this unique book, science meets self-discovery."

- Peter McKnoulty, Transition Planning, Australia

"This is one of the best self-help books I have ever read. It challenges you to look at yourself in a way you've never done before. It invites you into a conversation with a very important and special person- yourself.

There is a Latin adage, which translates literally as follows: "man is born free but wherever he goes he is always in chains". Jack Beauregard; using his personal life story and solid research has raised our awareness as to what may constitute these chains and more importantly offers us a road map to true freedom."

- Simon Aidoo, Director, Transition Planning,
United Kingdom

"I think this book will prove to be an extremely powerful and helpful tool for many people. I loved how the Self Discovery Checklist as I read the book – it tied in together nicely! Very positive and uplifting!"

- Sandra Munier, Esq. Phoenix, Arizona

Quotes of Why You Would Want to Live with Authenticity

"I had no idea that being your authentic self could make me rich as I've become. If I had, I'd have done it a lot earlier."

> \- Oprah Winfrey

"The privilege of a lifetime is to become who you truly are."

> \- Carl Jung

"This above all: to thine own self be true."

> \- W. Shakespeare, *Hamlet*

"To be what we are, and to become what we are capable of becoming, is the only end in life."

> \- Robert Louis Stevenson

"To be yourself in a world that is constantly trying to make you something else is the greatest accomplishment."

> \- Ralph Waldo Emerson

"You have the freedom to be yourself, your true self here and now, and nothing can stand in your way."

> \- Richard Bach, Jonathan

Also by the author

The Power of Balance:
Seven Principles for Transforming Mind, Spirit and Self

Finding Your New Owner:
For Your Business, For Your Life:
A Guide to a New Paradigm for
Baby Boomer Business Owners

7 PRINCIPLES

FOR LIVING WITH

AUTHENTICITY

Discovering Your True Self
When Facing Life Changes

Jack Beauregard

STPI Press
Cambridge, Massachusetts

Published by:
STPI Press
Cambridge, MA 02140
www.theplatinumyears.com

Beauregard, Jack

7 Principles For Living With Authenticity: Discovering Your True Self When Facing Life Changes / Jack Beauregard / Cambridge MA / STPI Press, 2016.

Paperback:
ISBN-10: 0-9836311-6-6
ISBN-13: 978-0-9836311-6-3

Hardcover:
ISBN-10: 0-9836311-2-3
ISBN-13: 978-0-9836311-2-5

Printed in the United States of America, Australia and United Kingdom.

Table of Contents

Table of Contents

In gratitude to our True Selves who have created the desire in us to seek the truth.

Dedication

To Maureen: An incredibly intelligent, loving and compassionate human being - a Great Soul. I know that I am a very blessed man to have Maureen as my wife, my friend, and my soul mate, and thankful for her support over the past 23 years which has made my journey of self-discovery possible.

In Gratitude

To Barbra Brandt for her structural editing which greatly contributed to the writing of this book.

To Paul Cronin, my business partner, for spending the last seven years true to the message and for helping bring the Successful Transition Planning Institute's programs out to the world

To the readers of the original manuscript for their invaluable feedback: Peter McKnoulty, Dave Sinclair, Sandra Munier and Lois Andre, and to Andy Moysenko for his scientific clarification of the book and his support over the years.

To all of the people who have been trained to be Transition Planning Consultants and Transition Advisors, as well as many professionals who shared our ideals with their clients over the years.

To the design and project management team at Lipstick Marketing for designing the cover for the book and for years of excellent service.

Foreword

Larry Gard, Ph.D., Consulting Psychologist

The term *identity crisis* has become so much a part of our vernacular that we occasionally fail to grasp the magnitude of its emotional impact. As a consulting psychologist, I see how profoundly experiencing an identity crisis impacts my clients who are going through personal and business-related transitions.

Many people fear that if they leave their business or profession they will lose their identity. Who we are is intimately tied to what we do. Feeling threatened by a perceived loss of identity, we may avoid thinking about difficult topics such as "What will happen to me after I leave?" and at a deeper level, "What will happen to the *memory* of me?" As a result, we may continue to work—by default and sometimes against our own interests—because we're unwilling or unable to grapple with these issues.

Thinking about the next chapter in your life forces you to face profound questions about what is genuinely important to you and what you want to do next. When making decisions about their lives, my clients fare best when they are true to themselves, as they learn how to uncover essential values and acknowledge what is most meaningful to them. This process requires a significant degree of self-awareness. By analogy, you can probably combyour hair while staring out the window, but chances are, you'll achieve far better results with a mirror. In this book the author, Jack Beauregard, has carefully laid out a self-reflective process that helps foster the reader's heightened self-awareness.

One of the things that I've long admired about Jack is his ability to translate complex concepts into ideas that are readily grasped, meaningful, and relevant. In *7 Principles for Living with Authenticity*, Jack has tackled an incredibly daunting task. By sharing his own journey of self-discovery, he has crafted an accessible guide to help readers discern their authentic identities.

This book's System for Self-Discovery is based on seven high-level principles, each one associated with a specific step toward connecting to your true self. For example, Jack describes the Principle of Centeredness and the notion that we can connect to the innate wisdom of our inner self. He presents the various reasons why we lose touch with our inner core, eventually failing to recognize and respect our feelings. And he describes methodologies for reconnecting to one's inner core.

With the Principle of Wholeness, Jack conveys the importance of honoring and integrating all parts of yourself—positive and negative, inner and outer, head and heart. He cautions against believing that we're made up of pairs of disconnected opposites, one pole superior and the other inferior. My work affirms that balance is critical, and sometimes there are multiple elements in play. For example, most of us are consciously aware of our thoughts, feelings, and behaviors, but it is rare for people to give all three areas equal attention. Yet ignoring any one of these three can have a negative impact on our decisions and our relationships. This book can help the reader connect to all three aspects of oneself.

In another chapter, Jack introduces the Principle of Association, the notion that "seeming opposites are connected by a continuum." He explains that we can expand our options in life by considering what exists between two extremes. This reminds me of one of my clients who struggled with a rather black or white, all-or nothing worldview. In a moment of recognition, he quipped, "I guess if it wasn't for gray areas, I couldn't order my steak medium rare!"

Don't worry if you find yourself unable to complete some of the exercises in this book, or if at the end you feel that certain matters remain unclear. If you feel mildly unsettled, don't be discouraged; it probably indicates that you are beginning to wrestle with some deep and important questions. Just

Remember that the journey inward is not swift or direct, nor is it always comfortable, but the process itself—and your discoveries along the way—will undoubtedly add meaning to your life.

Larry Gard, Ph.D.
President, Hamilton-Chase Consulting
Chicago, Il

Introduction: The Freedom to Be Who You Really Are

- Do you want to live an authentic life?

- Are you someone who has been successful in your work life, but now you're wondering "Who am I?"

- Are you going through a major life transition, and you want to be true to yourself in the next chapter of your life?

If you answered Yes to any of these questions, then this book is for you.

The journey to authenticity

When I was the CEO of Designer Orthopedics, a multi-million dollar medical supply company I founded in the 1980s, I looked like a winner—but something important was missing from my life. I realized that I could not feel genuinely fulfilled or satisfied until I discovered who I truly was, so I could live more authentically.

Through my own journey of self-discovery, I was able to connect to my True Self. I then created a method that other people with backgrounds similar to mine could use, so they could effectively and systematically make the journey to their own authenticity, wholeness, and genuine fulfillment.

For over 25 years, through the two companies I founded—Innervisions Associates and the Successful Transition Planning Institute—I've developed and presented my unique approach to help thousands of people examine and reframe their lives so they too could become more self-aware and more authentically happy and successful. The people I've worked with include professionals in medicine, health care, social services, education, law, and information technology; and advisors who provide owners and other successful individuals with professional services in financial planning, wealth management, organizational development and business growth.

The Successful Transition Planning Institute is now an internationally-recognized thought leader in the field of personal and business transition planning, with STPI-certified Transition Planning Consultants and Transition Advisors on four continents—in the United States, Canada, the United Kingdom, South Africa, and Australia. Using the unique methodology I developed, my colleagues and I at STPI specialize in helping professionals, executives, and business owners experience personal growth, plan and implement successful personal and business transitions, and create new lives that they cannot wait to live.

This book presents the system I developed to help people discover and live from their own True Selves. Do the following characteristics describe you?

- You like to work hard.
- You value yourself for your accomplishments.
- You want to be successful in whatever you do, and you enjoy the rewards that come with success.
- Your work is important to you. (It can easily become the most important part of your life.)
- You know how to get things done, and you are inspired by having a goal or purpose.

If this sounds like you, then this book is for you.

Why you might face an Identity Crisis, and how to benefit from it

Your personal identity affects the way you think, and feel about yourself, and has a strong impact on your level of self-esteem. Your personal identity needs to change as your life circumstances change. People who experience a major life-transition are often thrown into an Identity Crisis, as all your old rules, roles, and sources of support have suddenly evaporated. Here are some of the life-transitions that might generate an Identity Crisis in your life:

- A mid-life crisis
- Divorce
- Loss of a loved one
- Experiencing Empty Nest Syndrome
- When letting go of an addiction
- Leaving your professional career
- Being let go from your job
- Surviving a life threatening experience
- No longer owning a business
- Retiring

Going through any of these transitions can cause you to ask yourself: "Who am I when I'm no longer doing what I currently do?" Even though this crisis causes significant upheaval, it also provides you with the opportunity to rediscover who you really are, so you can rethink and reframe your life.

Even if no major changes are taking place in your life and things appear to be going well, you may still feel that something is not right about your life. For whatever reason, you may be going through an existential crisis that motivates you to start asking the big questions, such as "What is my purpose in life?" "Do I really matter?" or "Who am I really?"

If you are going through a life-transition or facing an Identity Crisis for whatever reason, you need to expand your definition of who you are beyond what you are doing and discover and connect to your True Self, so you can live the next chapter of your life from the goals, values, and passions of who you really are.

Breaking free from your False Self: How this book can help you connect to your True Self

Each person's True Self is unique. Because each of us is different, your True Self will include your own unique gifts and talents, goals, values, experiences, work style, and more.

Through the System for Self-Discovery described in this book, you begin your journey of connecting to your own unique True Self by recognizing that until now, you've been held back because you've been trying to live from a False Self. This book explains why we create a False Self, how our False Self holds us back, and how by using the System for Self-Discovery, you, too, can gain the freedom of becoming who you really are.

Many of us are now realizing that we've been trying to live from an image of who we thought we were "supposed to" be, instead of being who we really are. This image that we want to present to the world is often one of unblemished perfection and success. You may have developed this self-image because you wanted other people to like you, or because you believed that in order to be successful you had to present a perfect image to others, or you wanted to appear flawless in order to blot out aspects of yourself that you felt were unacceptable. But whatever the reason, many people are realizing that this False Self-Image no longer works for them.

I compare the False Self to a cocoon that has held you imprisoned for many years, with your True Self as a butterfly that is getting ready to emerge from this cocoon. In order to break free and fly high, you need to break free from the limitations of your False Self.

Becoming your True Self does not happen overnight. It is a process that takes time and effort. However, you already know how to work hard, and you've already demonstrated your ability to succeed throughout your life. Now you can apply these abilities to the process of breaking free from your False Self, and discovering and living from your True Self.

The System for Self-Discovery which I developed, and that this book presents, is a logical, businesslike, step-by-step method specifically designed for people like you—people who work hard and enjoy being successful. This system is also based on the latest discoveries in many areas of science— from cosmology to neuroscience (brain science). The

System for Self-Discovery consists of seven principles that will help you connect to your True Self. Each chapter explains how one of these principles can help you discover who you really are, and includes a set of exercises through which you apply that principle in your own life. With each new chapter, you gain new abilities that will help your True Self more fully emerge from that cocoon, so you can fly freely.

Are you ready to begin your own journey of self-discovery?

Are you excited by the possibility of breaking free from the limiting cocoon of your False Self, and connecting to who you really are, so you can live more authentically? If your answer is Yes—then let's begin the journey!

*****

Chapter 1.

From False Self to True Self: Discovering Who You Really Are

When I was the CEO of Designer Orthopedics, a multi-million dollar medical supply company I founded in the 1980s, I looked like a winner but I felt like a fraud.

From the outside, I was the person who "had it all," who "had it made." I looked like a winner because I had all the external trappings of success—the money, the position, the clothes, the family, the house, the boat, the cars. But inside I was empty. Something was missing from my life.

Despite my success, negative voices kept popping up in my head, telling me:

"I'm not good enough."

"I'm really a failure."

"I can't do this."

"What's wrong with me?"

I was living on an emotional roller coaster—either completely up, positive and self-confident, or deeply down, negative and depressed. I had built a façade of perfection around myself that I worked hard to maintain. I didn't want anyone to know about the times when I'd failed to live up to my image of perfection and success. In fact, I tried to keep thoughts about my occasional failures out of my own consciousness, so I could maintain this totally positive, successful image of myself.

I didn't know where all that negative, critical self-talk was coming from, but those negative voices hit home. Inside, I actually felt like a fraud and a hypocrite, and I was constantly anxious and worried that people would find out I really was a fraud. It felt like a civil war was raging inside me.

The façade of my False Self

Before I could help others, I first had to take my own journey of self-discovery. My path to authenticity began when I realized that the person I was projecting to the world around me was actually a "False Self," and my commitment to keeping up this False Self-Image was preventing me from becoming who I really was.

This book describes what I've learned over the years about why we create a False Self, how our False Self holds us back, and how you can use the System for Self-Discovery that I developed, so you too can gain the freedom of becoming who you really are.

Moving beyond my False Self

In order to be successful, I had developed a façade of perfection and success that I projected to the world around me, but inside that façade I was deeply unhappy. Only when a personal crisis forced me to begin looking within, did I realize that I was living from a False Self. I realized that in order to feel better about myself, I had to reconnect to and live from my True Self. But what was my True Self? Who was I, really? And how could I bring my True Self more fully into my life?

I went on a personal quest to discover my True Self. I took graduate courses at Harvard Divinity School, hoping that the wisdom of the world's religions might help me. Like many people who value success and self-improvement, I also read numerous self-help books, attended self-help seminars and listened to countless self-help tapes, which all advised me to "think positively." But the negative voices inside of me did not go away. I kept asking myself, "What is wrong with me?" In fact, I often felt worse after reading positive self-help books, since I agreed with what they were saying, yet I still did negative things.

Finally I realized that I would have to create my own path for discovering my True Self. Much of what I did to rediscover and reconnect to my True Self I did by trial-and-error, guided by instinct and intuition. Also during this time I began reading about new ways of looking at reality, based on the latest scientific discoveries about the universe and ourselves, and these new scientific perspectives expanded my thinking and gave me a new approach for understanding myself and my place in the universe.

After several years of working in this way, I realized that something in me was different. My life had actually changed.

- My feelings about myself had changed, because I now really liked myself.
- My relationships had changed for the better.
- I felt more genuine. I was now making choices and decisions from my own authentic values.

Somehow I had connected to, and was now living from, my True Self.

The two walls that kept me imprisoned within my False Self

During my journey of self-discovery, I became aware that I had created two mental walls—one wall around me, the other inside of me—that were preventing me from connecting to my True Self. On the outside was the façade of my False Self—the image of absolute perfection and success that I tried to live up to, and that I constantly projected to the world around me.

On the inside was a second wall that prevented me from knowing who I really was. This internal wall was constructed of beliefs about myself—such as my beliefs that in reality I was a terrible person, that I was inadequate, unworthy, and did not deserve to be happy or successful. (See Figure 1.)

Figure 1.
The two walls that were preventing me from connecting to my True Self

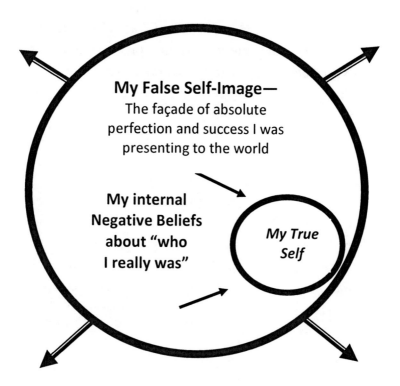

My False Self-Image—
The façade of absolute perfection and success I was presenting to the world

My internal Negative Beliefs about "who I really was"

My True Self

One reason I had created that external façade around myself was because I was afraid that if people could see who I really was, they would no longer respect or like me. So my external façade was designed to impress people—but it also kept people away.

Because I had learned that success depends on always being positive, it was difficult for me to accept that I actually had so many negative beliefs about myself. In fact, because these negative beliefs and feelings of worthlessness were so painful, for most of my life I had hidden them below my conscious awareness—I had buried them deep in my unconscious mind, and I had built a wall around them in order to keep them out of my conscious awareness. Nevertheless, my negative self-image kept coming through in that negative, critical self-talk that so often popped up in my mind.

My life felt like an emotional roller coaster because I kept jumping back and forth between two extremes. On the one hand, I was trying to live up to my external self-image of grandiosity, over-achievement, total perfection and success. But on the other hand, deep inside I had somehow picked up—and accepted—the beliefs that I was really a terrible, weak, worthless person.

In reality, I was neither of these two extremes. I realized that in order to become my True Self so I could live more authentically, I would have to dissolve both my external façade of total perfection and my internal wall of false negative beliefs about myself.

Creating a System for Self-Discovery

After I had connected to my own True Self, I realized I had to create a method that other people could use, so they could effectively and systematically do what I had done—make the journey to their own authenticity, wholeness, and genuine fulfillment. I developed my System for Self-Discovery, which allowed me to create a new career for myself doing what I truly wanted—sharing my discoveries about the False Self and helping other people connect to their own unique True Selves. For over 25 years I've shared this System for Self-Discovery through one-on-one counseling, by presenting conference keynotes, workshops, and other speaker presentations, through training programs for advisors and coaches, and through products such as my books and internet-based educational programs.

I felt more fulfilled as I met other successful professionals, business owners, executives, and advisors who were also looking for the connection between success, happiness, and authenticity—people who found my message and my new work valuable. I was connecting to and working with people I liked and respected, people who inspired me, and who appreciated and supported the new work I was doing.

Learning about the latest discoveries in many areas of science helped me realize that there were seven scientifically-validated principles I had instinctively used in my own journey of self-discovery—principles that other people could now consciously apply in order to reconnect to their True Selves. These seven principles are the foundation of the System for Self-Discovery and the core of this book.

Benefits and Limitations of the False Self

There are certainly advantages to be gained by living from a False Self-Image and projecting it to the world around you.

- Your False Self-Image helps you be successful because you appear to other people like you have confidence, like you have your act together and you are a winner.
- Because your False Self keeps you externally focused on your work and accomplishments, you don't have to look too closely at the thoughts and feelings going on inside you.
- If you have negative emotions about yourself, telling yourself that you are your perfect False Self-Image helps

you avoid thinking about or feeling these negative emotions.

At the same time, there are also drawbacks to trying to live from your False Self.

- If you feel that you are not really this ideal self-image that you are presenting to the world, then you feel like a fraud and a hypocrite.

- Trying to maintain your False Self contributes to anxiety, because you worry that people will find out that you really are a fraud.

- Because your False Self is supported by external accomplishments such as achievement, status, and success, if you lose any of these, then you lose your identity.

- It requires a lot of time and energy to keep your False Self-Image in place.

- You may be avoiding close relationships or genuine intimacy, because you are afraid that if people get to know you, they will find out who you really are—and because who you really are is flawed and imperfect, they will no longer respect or like you.

Do any of these issues sound familiar?

Where did our False Self come from?

Much of our False Self-Image comes from limiting beliefs about ourselves and the world—beliefs that we learned from our parents and teachers while growing up, and also that we learned as adults, from our work environment and the prevailing larger culture. These limiting beliefs include:

- Beliefs about who we really are
- Beliefs about the types of goals we can achieve
- Beliefs about how the world works, and about the nature of the universe and our role in it
- Beliefs about our power to change ourselves and our lives

Many of these limiting beliefs are conscious. For example, the statement that "It's good to always think positively, to always be positive" is a well-known belief that most of us accept—but as you will see, the belief that we must always be positive can actually limit you and prevent you from connecting to a more authentic life. We also hold many limiting beliefs without being consciously aware of them. Both types of limiting beliefs contribute to our False Self, and prevent us from becoming our True Self.

The idea that "You gain your identity from your work, and you can measure your worth by what—and how much—you accomplish" is another familiar assumption that most of us take for granted;

however, this belief also prevents us from becoming who we really are.

So the System for Self-Discovery helps you recognize and consider the impact of your consciously-held beliefs that are preventing you from connecting to your True Self.

We also carry around many limiting beliefs that we are not consciously aware of—unconscious beliefs about ourselves, how the world works, and what we think is possible; yet our unconscious beliefs also have an extremely powerful impact on us. The System for Self-Discovery also helps you become aware of limiting beliefs you may not realize you have.

Our False Self came from limiting emotional patterns and behaviors we developed in response to how we were treated when we were growing up, starting with our earliest years. Because these emotional patterns and behaviors are so ingrained in us, we tend to fall back on them automatically even if they do not support our most effective performance and full development. The System for Self-Discovery helps you recognize the limiting emotional patterns and behaviors that are preventing you from creating a genuinely successful and fulfilling life.

The larger cultural systems in which we were raised and in which we live also contribute to the creation of our False Self. For example, most of us were raised in the Mechanistic Paradigm—a worldview based in Newtonian science, which says that the universe is a rigidly structured world made up of material objects, such as the planets and our own bodies, which react when they are influenced by physical forces like gravity and inertia. This Mechanistic cosmology teaches us to view the universe as meaningless dead matter and to view ourselves as tiny meaningless specks in a dead, meaningless universe.[1] This Mechanistic view can cause us to feel a deep sense of personal insignificance, believing that our lives are senseless and have no purpose.

The System for Self-Discovery presents a dynamic new view of the universe and our role in it, based on the latest scientific discoveries.[2]

Discovering your True Self

We may avoid acknowledging that we are living from a False Self-Image because we feel we have no alternative. This is who we are, this is how we have to live, we don't know how to change things, or the idea of trying to live differently is overwhelming.

So it's important for you to remember that who you really are never left you; you simply got into the habit of not being aware of its existence deep inside you. Your True Self has been trying to connect with you over the years, as expressed by your desire to become the person you know you could be.

Feelings of inner emptiness are another way your True Self has been trying to tell you that it was missing in your life.

Even though each of us is different, I've learned over the years that there are several basic qualities needed in order to connect to your True Self. Becoming your True Self does not happen overnight. Like any project that you commit yourself to accomplishing, discovering who you really are is a process that takes time. Discovering your True Self requires you to establish goals, then take the steps needed to achieve these goals. However, you already know how to work hard, and you've already demonstrated your ability to succeed throughout your life. Now you can apply these abilities to the process of discovering and living from your True Self.

The process of successfully connecting to your True Self requires the following:

1. Having the <u>desire and motivation</u> to want to connect to your True Self, so you can live more authentically.

2. Having the <u>curiosity</u> to want to discover who your True Self really is.

3. Knowing that genuine change is <u>possible</u>, and that you have the <u>power</u> to create the necessary changes in your life.

4. Being willing to <u>recognize and acknowledge</u> the limiting beliefs and emotions that are preventing you from living authentically.

5. Having the <u>courage</u> to explore your own limiting beliefs and emotions.

6. Understanding that you can <u>transform</u> your limiting beliefs and emotional patterns by recognizing their origins, recognizing how they are holding you back, and being willing to <u>replace</u> these limiting beliefs and emotional patterns with more supportive and authentic new beliefs and behaviors.

7. Being willing to <u>keep practicing</u> your new beliefs and new, more genuine ways of acting on a regular basis, since (as the latest discoveries in brain science tell us) it takes time to change your brain, and we have to repeat a new action many times until it becomes an innate part of us.

Moving from your False to your True Self

Figure 2. Your False and Your True Self

How your False Self-Image holds you back and limits you	The freedom of living from your True Self
Intellectual limitations of the False Self: • Thinks rigidly and narrowly • Always has to appear "positive" • Uses All-or-Nothing, Black-or-White thinking	Intellectual advantages of your True Self: • Thinks more effectively and creatively • Can see both the upsides and the downsides of any issue

• Jumps between two opposite extremes	• Sees a range of options and possibilities in any situation • Sees change as a step-by-step process
The False Self causes you to have a limited identity: • Externally oriented • Always has to impress or please other people • Identifies with your roles and external accomplishments • Lacks an authentic foundation for making choices and taking action • Divides you into disconnected parts • Overemphasizes some of your aspects • Ignores, represses, or denies other aspects of yourself	**Your True Self allows you to live from your whole, genuine identity—you can:** • Identify with your own unique individual self • Make choices and take action based on what you really value • Recognize, acknowledge, and integrate all aspects of yourself • Use all of your abilities, gifts, and talents • Feel more complete

Emotional limitations of the False Self:	Your True Self brings more love into your life, because you:
• Feel unworthy of love • Not able to love yourself • Has difficulty giving love to other people • Avoids genuine intimacy	• Know you are worthy of love • Can feel healthy self-love • Can fully love other people • Can create genuinely fulfilling relationships and intimacy
A limited (and limiting) Belief System, causes you to:	An expanded, empowering Belief System, causes you to:
• Feel trapped by old negative beliefs • Be easily thrown off course by negative circumstances • Become overwhelmed by change • Believe that only external circumstances make you feel important • Feel disconnected from your own genuine sources of meaning and purpose	• Recognize your innate power to create effective change • Stay centered, no matter what • Transform negative circumstances (past, present, and future) into positive outcomes • Connect to your own inner sources of meaning and purpose • Know that your life is innately important

Why your False Self cannot bring you genuine happiness and success

There are many ways in which a person's False Self-Image holds them back from genuine success and fulfillment.

• An External orientation—believing that you are your accomplishments

Like many of us, I was brought up to believe that success could be measured according to external criteria such as status, power and possessions, and that winning was the key to success. Competition was my way of life. I loved engaging in the challenge, strategizing and doing whatever had to be done in order to win. Competition focused and energized me around the only thing that mattered in my life— winning. However, this competitive attitude was preventing me from having truly fulfilling relationships with other people.

A core belief of the False Self is that you are your accomplishments, and are valued according to your accomplishments. Take away your accomplishments, and you have no value. Accomplishing things and winning can certainly bring you happiness, at least temporarily; but ultimately your feelings of self-worth have to come from within. In order to live authentically, you have to discover that your True Self is more than your external accomplishments.

● Overemphasis on achievement causes you to feel intrinsically unimportant

If you identify yourself with your achievements, then you are valued only for what you can achieve. You are important only as long as you keep on achieving. Your life is important only as long as you keep on achieving.

You need a more authentic basis for feeling that you and your life are truly important.

● Extreme Perfectionism

When I was living from my False Self, I was an extreme perfectionist, as are many of the people I've worked with.

There's nothing wrong with having high standards, being good with details, and taking the time to do a job well, if you can also recognize that making mistakes is part of the process and you can learn from your mistakes. But that's not who I was. Being an extreme perfectionist means that you always have to be totally perfect, period. Unfortunately, the flip side of extreme perfectionism is that no matter how hard you try, you can never quite measure up to the absolute standards you've set for yourself. If you make even one mistake—if you fail even once—then you consider yourself a total failure. Does that sound familiar?

You can become so preoccupied with trying to be perfect that you miss the positive benefits generated by mistakes. Mistakes are a form of feedback, but the perfectionist is so busy responding to the self-critical voices in their own head that it's difficult for them to pay attention to this feedback communicated by their mistakes, and as a result they can't learn from their mistakes, or they can't shift out of a poorly-chosen course of action.

Ironically, extreme perfectionism actually holds you back from taking action. When faced with a project they have to accomplish, extreme perfectionists procrastinate, because they are so afraid of making a mistake.

You may feel that your perfectionism is simply part of who you are; but if you are an extreme perfectionist, this characteristic actually prevents you from being as successful as you might be, and it can bring much anguish and anxiety into your life. The good news is that because extreme perfectionism is part of the False Self, you can transform it by reconnecting to your True Self. (See Chapter 9.)

- **Trying to be your False Self prevents you from being a whole person**

Our False Self-Image overemphasizes a few limited aspects of ourselves, especially our work and our striving for status and material success, while it ignores, represses, or denies other parts of ourselves—such as our need for love, intimate relationships, leisure, play, and other non-work-related aspects of oneself.

But you can't really feel happy and fulfilled if parts of yourself are being ignored or denied.

- **The limited thinking style of the False Self limits your effectiveness**

Because your False Self-Image requires that you always think, talk, feel, and act positive, it prevents you from seeing the whole picture, and actually limits your ability to develop options and choices.

Limited thinking limits your effectiveness. The limited thinking style of the False Self prevents you from seeing the full range of possibilities, which limits your ability to make decisions and act effectively. Over the years I've seen many examples of how an exclusive focus on the positive caused business owners to make personal and business decisions that were doomed to fail, or led them to take unsuccessful approaches to transitioning into the next chapter of their lives.

Living from your True Self allows you to expand your thinking, so you can become more creative and effective, and make more successful decisions.

- **Constant worry about what other people will think**

Because the purpose of the False Self is to constantly impress or be pleasing and acceptable to other people, when you live from your False Self-Image, you are always worrying about the impression you make on other people.

True self-confidence comes from feeling comfortable with yourself and your own inner values, instead of constantly trying to shape your life according to other people's criteria.

- **The False Self prevents you from bringing love fully into your life**

Overemphasis on your work limits the time and energy available for your family, and your focus on achievement can carry over into your family and other personal relationships, distorting how you relate to other people. For example, you might value the people close to you only for their achievements and express love for them only if they live up to your excessively high standards, rather than loving them for who they are.

Trying to maintain a False Self-Image also means you are afraid that if other people get too close, they will find out "who you really are"—which includes your hidden negative aspects. This prevents authentic relationships and genuine intimacy, because you can't share your whole self with other people.

Living from your True Self allows you to bring authentic love and genuine relationships into your life.

The System for Self-Discovery: A systematic methodology for living from your True Self

While I was on my own journey of self-exploration and discovery, I was also reading about dynamic new worldviews based on the latest scientific discoveries in fields such as cosmology, astronomy, physics, ecology, biology, medicine and health care, mathematics, information technology, and brain science (neuroscience).

In contrast to the static, materialistic worldview of the Mechanistic Paradigm, these new scientific discoveries are revealing that we live in an ever-evolving universe; each of us is personally connected to the dynamic forces and creative patterns of the universe; how we think influences the reality we experience; and by changing how we think and act, we can literally "rewire" our own brains and change who we truly are.[3]

The System for Self-Discovery presented in this book brings together and applies many of these new scientific discoveries to help you move beyond your False Self, so you can rediscover and live from your own unique True Self.

Change your beliefs, change your life

The System for Self-Discovery emphasizes changing your beliefs about yourself and the world. Understanding how powerfully your beliefs shape your reality, and realizing that as you change your beliefs, you can change your life experiences, is key to your self-discovery and the creation of a fulfilling new life.

If you believe something is possible, you will try to achieve it, while if you believe that something is not possible, then you will not bother attempting to make it happen. For example, if you believe that your future will be boring and meaningless, you will do everything possible to stay where you are now in life. In both positive and negative ways, your beliefs create your model of the world and what you think is possible in it.

The concept that your beliefs create your reality has now been well documented. It is applied in psychology, medicine, even in business and sales training, and many books and seminars teach how to apply this concept for success in business or for personal growth and empowerment.[4]

Numerous examples demonstrate how what we believe can actually create our personal physical reality. For example, during a football game in Monterey Park, California in 1982, four spectators had to leave their seats because of severe nausea and dizziness. These four individuals had all drunk soda from one specific dispensing machine. Out of concern that the water or syrup in all the dispensing machines might be contaminated, officials made a public announcement requesting that no one consume any soft drinks from the beverage-dispensing machines until the precise cause of that sudden illness could be ascertained. Upon hearing this, numerous spectators throughout the stadium suddenly started retching and fainting, and 191 people had to be transported to local hospitals, where emergency-room physicians reported that they all had genuine symptoms of food poisoning. (Surprisingly, all these people who became ill in response to the public announcement quickly made a complete recovery.) Subsequent laboratory analysis of the components of the soda in the rest of the stadium showed that there was nothing wrong with it.[5] It seems that these hundreds of fans believed so strongly that they might have drunk poisoned soda, that their bodies produced the actual physical symptoms of food poisoning, even though their soda was in fact untainted.

In another example, 150 medical students were given various psychotropic drugs. Half of the students were told they were receiving a tranquilizer, while the other half were told they were receiving an antidepressant. In actuality, the group who thought they were getting the tranquilizer received the antidepressant, and the group who thought they were getting the antidepressant actually received the tranquilizer. In more than half of the cases, the students showed symptoms which reflected what they thought they had been given![6] For these students, their power of belief was so strong that it not only overcame the effect of the actual ingredients in the medications they had received; their beliefs actually produced physical symptoms that matched what they assumed they had been given.

A third example provides a dramatic demonstration of how our beliefs can create limiting mental "walls" that restrict our actions. I saw this in a video of a large fish—a Northern pike—that was put into a spacious fish tank, then a smaller fish tank was inverted and placed over the pike. Tiny minnows—the pike's natural food—were then placed in the water just outside the inverted tank. Every time that pike went to feed on those minnows, it would hit the glass walls of the inverted tank. The more it kept trying, the more it would hit those walls. After a while, the smaller tank was removed, allowing the pike to swim out to catch the minnows; however, that pike stayed within the confines of the previous barrier. It believed that those walls were still there,

57

even though they were now gone. The pike was starving, and its food was swimming all around it, but it couldn't move out beyond its self-imposed walls to get what it needed.[7]

Our own limiting mental walls prevent us from seeing a whole new world of possibilities. These limitations have been created in us through beliefs such as "I can't do that" or "This is impossible." Showing you how to expand your mind beyond limiting assumptions and how to create new alternatives and beliefs, the System for Self-Discovery that I developed will help you actualize your fullest potential and help you successfully make any life transitions you may be facing.

The Power of Courage, the Power to Change, and the Power to Choose

The System for Self-Discovery brings three gifts to assist you in becoming your True Self. First is the Power of Courage, a power which is inherently yours. The System for Self-Discovery will help you develop a strong belief in yourself, creating the courage which enables you to stand up to whatever difficulties you may face while exploring your inner self and creating a new life. Courage provides you with the freedom to go beyond your fears so that you can test your limits, break through barriers, and move to places you have never been before. The System for Self-Discovery provides you with the courage to make meaningful changes in your life.

This courageous attitude brings a second gift: the Power to Change, which allows you to realize that you no longer have to do the "same old, same old," that there are new ways to live. Through the System for Self-Discovery, you begin to see a whole new spectrum of alternatives, an expanded range of options for yourself and your life. The Power to Change allows you to move beyond what you previously believed to be the "old you." As you realize that you can be different, the System for Self-Discovery will help you transform your life.

An expanded awareness of alternatives brings the third gift: the Power to Choose, because you have the fundamental right to choose how your life will be. The Power to Choose awakens your power to make your own decisions, rather than letting other people make decisions for you. Your choices create your life, and the Power to Choose will help you make the choices that allow you to live more authentically.

The System for Self-Discovery can provide you with the power that is inherently yours as a human being to choose how you want to spend the rest of your life. It will help you open your life to gifts and opportunities far greater than you could ever have created through your limited, isolated False Self.

*****

Chapter 2.

The System for Self-Discovery: Seven Principles for Connecting to Your True Self

As I worked on my own process of self-discovery, I realized that there are newly discovered scientific principles that apply both to the universe in its largest manifestation and also to my personal experience as a person seeking meaningful self-transformation and a fulfilling way of living. I developed seven principles based on these new scientific discoveries to create the System for Self-Discovery.

The System for Self-Discovery

The System for Self-Discovery is a powerful methodology you can use in order to discover and begin living from your own True Self. This system allows you to effectively and systematically make the journey to your own authenticity, wholeness, and genuine fulfillment.

This System for Self-Discovery is a step-by-step methodology that builds on itself. Each new Principle guides you in going deeper and adds new abilities as you take your own journey to authenticity. This system shows you how to expand the way you think, so you can broaden your view of who you are, what is possible for you, and can increase the options and choices available for creating a more authentic life.

Through this seven-step process you will learn how to eliminate or transform barriers that are holding you back from achieving genuine fulfillment and success, while increasing your abilities and developing the skills you need in order to achieve your authentic goals. Using these seven scientifically-based principles, you will:

- Move beyond an over simplistic "All-or-Nothing" view of yourself and the world, and gain the ability to deal more effectively with complexity.

- Look at your beliefs about yourself, and transform faulty negative beliefs that are holding you back.

- Discover what is really important to you, which provides a foundation on which you can create an authentically happy and successful life.

- Learn how to develop and use all your abilities, gifts and talents, so you can respond more effectively to discouragements, setbacks, and other challenges that arise in the course of life.

- Learn how to create authentic meaning and purpose in your life.

A scientifically-grounded methodology for connecting to your True Self

What you believe about the nature of the universe and your place in it is not a trivial matter, since it has profound consequences for how you think about yourself and all aspects of life. Your concept of the universe is important since it provides the framework which determines if you view yourself as significant or insignificant, and it creates the context for how you live your life.

In contrast to the static, materialistic worldview of the Mechanistic Paradigm, the latest scientific discoveries are revealing that we live in an ever-evolving universe; each of us is personally connected with the dynamic forces and creative patterns of the universe; how we think influences the reality we experience; and by changing how we think and act, we can literally "rewire" our own brains and change who we truly are.

Until very recently, our worldview of reality was shaped by the Mechanistic Paradigm, which began about 400 years ago at the end of the Renaissance.[8] The structure of the Mechanistic Paradigm was developed out of the principles developed by Isaac Newton. The machine imagery of

63

the Mechanistic Paradigm is reflected in how we describe ourselves and our work. For example, when a person is busy thinking, we often say that we "can hear the wheels turning," or we may say that someone has "an iron heart" or "a cast-iron stomach." Many people (including many medical professionals) view our bodies as the workings of a machine. We often describe our work as "putting our nose to the grindstone."

This machine imagery has affected how we live our lives. For example, machines do not have feelings, and many people also do not experience genuine feelings. The assumption that nothing is supposed to go wrong with a machine is often applied by the many people who believe that nothing should ever go wrong in their lives, no matter what they are involved in.

The purpose of machines is to produce, and many of us also believe that the sole purpose of our lives is to produce. Many companies view maintenance on machines as a downtime cost, and many people also view time not spent producing as a total waste of their time.

In the Mechanistic Paradigm, we were conditioned into the belief that we were insignificant in the vast void of a static empty universe. But a new cosmic perspective, emerging out of recent scientific discoveries, helps you become aware of the fact that you are inherently significant, because you are an active participant in the unfolding story of creation.

The universe supports your transformation

The Mechanistic or Newtonian view of the universe describes a rigidly structured world made up of material objects, such as the planets or our own bodies, which react when they are influenced by physical forces like gravity and inertia. By contrast, recent scientific discoveries have shown that we live in a dynamic universe, characterized by numerous coherent systems—be they galaxies, planets, bacteria, plants, animals, or human beings—each in the process of changing and being transformed. The universe is, in effect, a process of continual change, with new order arising out of chaos.[9] And you have the power to consciously participate in this natural process.

A central principle I learned during my journey to my True Self is that change is possible. Change is a natural part of life—in fact, both the universe and our own brains and bodies are characterized by ongoing change.

Our own human body is a marvelous expression of continual change, regeneration, and renewal. The lining of our stomach renews itself every four days; the outer layer of our skin renews itself every 35 days; we get a new liver every six weeks; our entire skeletal system replaces itself every three months; and the entire human body, down to the last atom, is replaced completely every five to seven years.[10]

I also learned from the latest discoveries in neuroscience that our brain has the innate capacity to change, learn, and grow at any age—a process called "neuroplasticity"—and that we can consciously increase our brain's abilities by changing how we think.[11] In fact, your entire brain replaces itself completely every two months![12] (This is what makes neuroplasticity possible.)

Neuroplasticity: Our brains constantly change and grow, and by changing how we think and act, we can change our own brains

The System for Self-Discovery emphasizes changing your beliefs about yourself and the world, because understanding how powerfully your beliefs shape your reality, and realizing that as you change your beliefs, you can change your life experiences, is key to your self-discovery and the creation of a fulfilling new life.

The concept that your beliefs create your reality has now been well documented. It is applied in psychology, medicine, even in business and sales training, and many books and seminars teach how to apply this concept for business success or personal empowerment and growth.[13]

Even more exciting, recent discoveries in brain science have revealed that we have the innate capacity to consciously "rewire" our own brains by changing how we think and act. Researchers have documented that you can consciously stimulate your brain's neuroplasticity to create extraordinary changes in your mental and emotional well-being, and to literally change your own life![14] For example, scientists have documented that you can consciously stimulate neuroplastic changes in your brain to:

- improve your physical, mental, and emotional well-being
- reduce depression, irritability, and stress disorders
- improve your effectiveness and success in school and at work
- improve your relationships with other people.

You may have heard that it takes 21 days of repeating a new habit to make it part of yourself; however, this popular belief is overly optimistic. Neuroscientists have now determined that in actuality, it generally takes anywhere from two months to eight months of regular practice to incorporate a new mental or behavioral pattern into your mind-brain-body system, although in some cases people were able to change an old habit in as quickly as 18 days.[15]

The System for Self-Discovery helps you utilize the neuroplastic potential of your brain to transform your beliefs and increase your abilities, so you can create a new, more genuine life for yourself.

Seven Principles for discovering your True Self

The System for Self-Discovery is based on three guiding tenets for you to keep in mind in order to fully live from your True Self.

- First, your True Self is waiting to be discovered.
- Second, your former self does not have to be your future self.
- And third, the more you live from who you really are, the more genuine fulfillment, happiness, success, and significance you will experience in your life.

Over the years, your authentic self has been attempting to align what you do with who you really are by creating a sense of longing, drawing you toward something unrecognized in your life. Experiencing satisfaction, peace of mind and happiness will inform you that what you are doing is in sync with your authentic self.

As I moved through my own process of self-discovery, I realized that there are seven principles—revealed by the latest scientific discoveries—that can help us become more fully connected to our True Selves. Some of these principles are about the universe in its largest manifestation, and at the same time apply to us as human beings connected to the universe. Other principles grow out of the latest findings in neuroscience. But all seven of these principles relate to your experience as a person seeking meaningful self-transformation and a fulfilling way of living.

I had instinctively used these seven principles in my own journey of self-discovery—and now I needed to put them into a system so other people could consciously apply them in order to reconnect to their True Selves and create more authentically happy and successful lives. I created a name for each Principle, and an explanation of how each Principle can be applied to help you discover and express your True Self. These Seven Principles are the foundation of the System for Self-Discovery and constitute the core of this book.

Applying the Seven Principles for Self-Discovery

Each of the following chapters focuses on, explains, and applies one of these Seven Principles. As you will see, each of the Principle's chapters follows the same format, and includes:

- A statement of the Principle described in that chapter
- A brief description of the False-Self problem addressed by that Principle
- A case study of how that Principle helped transform someone's life
- The scientific background for that Principle
- A discussion of why this False-Self problem develops, how to apply that Principle in your life, and the results and benefits of applying that Principle to help you become more fully your True Self

Each chapter ends with several exercises, including:

- An exercise to give you a general experience of that Principle
- One or more exercises through which you can apply that Principle specifically to your own life
- One or more exercises that help you continually practice this Principle in order to bring lasting neuroplastic changes in your brain and in your life

Each chapter of the Principles ends with a Checklist that helps you record your progress in applying the System for Self-Discovery, so you can see how far you have come in connecting to your True Self. This is followed by a summary box titled

"Seven Steps to Connect to Your True Self," which allows you to see how each new Principle brings you a new ability.

While you could read this entire book in one sitting, you will get the most value,and will better incorporate this material into your life, if you read this book on a day-to-day or week-to-week basis, and after reading each chapter, take the time to do the accompanying Exercises. By doing this, you will feel changes taking place in yourself and in your life, as you increasingly discover and connect to your own authenticity.

I congratulate you for being willing to embark on this significant journey!

*****

Chapter 3.

Expanding Your Thinking:
The Principle of Mutuality

Are you ready to learn a new way of thinking—a way that expands your thinking so you can more fully connect to and live from your True Self?

Principle #1, the Principle of Mutuality, introduces you to the dynamic results of Balanced Thinking.

---

1. The Principle of Mutuality

The universe is created and maintained through the dynamic balance of complementary opposites.

Application: If you have only one option, you can balance it by creating an opposite alternative to it. If one alternative appears positive and the other negative, expand your thinking by looking for the downsides in the positive aspect, and the upsides in the negative aspect; remember that every alternative has both positive and negative aspects.

Like many people who value success and self-improvement, I spent years trying to practice "positive thinking." But after reading positive self-help books, attending self-help seminars and listening to countless self-help tapes, I often felt worse, since I agreed with what they were saying, yet I still did negative things. As a result, I kept wondering "What's wrong with me?" I still had not achieved any fundamental changes in my personal life. I finally realized that trying to have an exclusive focus on the positive was actually limiting me.

I realized that if you focus exclusively on the positive, this decreases your effectiveness, because it prevents you from being aware of the whole picture. I also realized that my over attachment to positive thinking was an expression of a larger problem that characterized my False Self.

Discovering the Principle of Mutuality and applying it in my life was my first step toward my True Self. The more I used the Principle of Mutuality, the more I realized how this Principle can expand your view of yourself, and can help you become more effective and successful in your decisions and actions.

Helen A. was an attorney in mid-career, who needed to make some crucial personal and professional decisions. After I showed her the Principle of Mutuality, she applied it to her tendency of only looking at the positive upside of an issue. As she now understood that everything has both an upside and a downside, she was able to factor in not only the benefits, but also what might go wrong regarding each issue for which she was making a decision, and this helped her make better decisions for her work and her life.

The scientific basis for the Principle of Mutuality

The Principle of Mutuality is based on the latest scientific discoveries from physics and cosmology, which suggest that the universe is comprised of mutually complementary opposites. These interact and balance each other through processes of dynamic balance.[16]

A well-known example of dynamic balance exists at infinitely small levels, inside each atom: In every atom in the universe, the number of positively-charged protons within that atom's nucleus is balanced by exactly the same number of negatively-charged electrons orbiting around its nucleus.

Dynamic balance also fills the cosmos. In the Mechanistic Paradigm it was believed that space was a vacuum. The new cosmology shows us that space is actually filled with constantly fluctuating complementary energies—what looks to us like blackness in space is in reality made up of active complementary particles. In fact, the vacuum's seemingly totally empty space is actually a seething turmoil of creation and annihilation of matter-antimatter particle pairs.[17]

Most scientists today agree that the universe and everything in it came into being approximately 13.7 billion years ago with the Big Bang.[18] The very moment of the creation of the universe demonstrates the Principle of Mutuality, since during the first seconds following the Big Bang, the universe was filled with elementary subatomic particles and their antimatter complementary particles. Recent discoveries in physics also tell us that the universe is composed of both matter and antimatter. Antimatter is made of antiparticles, which have the same mass as ordinary matter, but opposite electrical charges. For example, the antiparticle complement to the negatively charged electron is the positively charged positron.[19]

Dynamic balance is also the basis for the life of every cell in your body, since in each cell there must be a constantly shifting balance between sodium and potassium electrolyte levels. In addition, each cell must maintain a delicate balance between internal and external pressure and electrolyte concentrations to avoid bursting or collapsing.[20]

Moving any part of your body also reflects complementarity. Each part of your body moves by "reciprocal inhibition," which means that, for example, as you move your arm away from your body, one set of muscles actively moves your arm away. A complementary set of muscles—which move your arm in toward your body—are temporarily suppressed, and only become active when you choose to move your arm back toward your body. This same phenomenon of reciprocal inhibition governs the movements of every part of your body.

Another example of the complementary nature of reality is the dynamic process that maintains balance between the number of species within a given area in ever-changing conditions. An example is the relationship between owls and their prey—mice—within a specific area. If the mouse population substantially increases, owls from other areas will move in and reduce the number of mice. When the original balance between the mouse and owl populations is reestablished, the owls from other territories will return home.[21]

The limits of Positive Thinking

Our False Self is one-dimensional. For example, the majority of us have been taught that if we just think positively, we will be happy and successful. Most of us accept this without question. Now there is nothing wrong with being positive; I would prefer to have a positive attitude or positive experiences rather than negative ones. Yet an absolute attachment to the positive can have a highly negative impact on how we think, perceive, and analyze the world around us.

My professional experience working with business owners and professionals who are going through transitions has provided numerous additional examples of how being over attached to positive thinking can limit us. Over the past two and half decades of working in the transition and transformational arenas, I have seen how an exclusive focus on the positive has caused many executives, professionals, and business owners to make personal and business decisions that were doomed to fail, or to take unsuccessful approaches to transitioning into the next stage of their lives.

Absolute Thinking

When I was living from my False Self, I engaged in a distorted way of thinking that is probably familiar to you, too. I call this thinking style "Absolute Thinking," also known as "All-or-Nothing" thinking.

Absolute Thinking causes us to see the world from an exclusively Black-or-White perspective, and to categorize situations as being either "all good" or "all bad." It causes us to view everyone and everything from a competitive point of view, because we have a zero-sum, I-win/You-lose approach to life. Because of its narrow perspective, Absolute Thinking makes us less effective in our decisions and actions. One example of Absolute, All-or-Nothing thinking is the belief that if you have any weaknesses at all, this means that you, yourself, are inherently weak—period (even though in reality you have both strengths and weaknesses).

Absolute Thinking is a one-dimensional way of thinking which says that there is only one alternative, only one way to be. Absolute Thinking is the limited thinking style of the False Self.

People who practice Absolute Thinking see only one possibility, or else they jump between two opposite extremes in their thinking. They see things as either "all Black" or "all White." They try to shove each of their experiences (including how they think about themselves and other people) into rigid categories by asking themselves "Is this good, or is it bad?" "Am I weak, or am I strong?" Because Absolute Thinking is such a limited way of relating to the world, people who are stuck in Absolute Thinking limit their effectiveness and their ability to make good decisions.

Expanding your thinking with Balanced Thinking

As I began my journey to my True Self, I realized that the one-dimensional approach of All-or-Nothing Absolute Thinking was keeping me stuck inside the walls of my False Self. To break free, I had to discover a more expanded and complex thinking style.

From reading about the latest discoveries in cosmology, I learned that reality is not one-dimensional, because the universe is created and maintained through the dynamic balance of complementary opposites. This inspired me to develop the first principle in the System for Self-Discovery—the Principle of Mutuality—and to apply this principle by developing a new, expanded thinking style that I call "Balanced Thinking."

The Principle of Mutuality expands your thinking by reminding you that everything has an opposite, so you do not have to be stuck with only one option. Furthermore, while Absolute Thinking says that something is either totally good or totally bad—either totally up or totally down—the Principle of Mutuality also says that everything has both positive and negative aspects—both upsides and downsides. (This helps you acknowledge the "Paradox of Extremes"—the fact that when anything good goes to extremes, it can have a negative consequence. For example, I think we would agree that love is good, but when, it goes too far, it can become smothering. Loyalty is also a good quality, but in the past when I became too loyal, it caused me to get stuck in situations I should have avoided.)

Here's how you can apply Balanced Thinking in your own life. Whenever you find yourself feeling stuck in a situation; or whenever you have to make a decision and you believe that you have only one choice, try this:

BALANCED THINKING

Step 1. To expand your thinking, create an opposite alternative to whatever seems like your only choice. You can now see both alternatives at the same time. (In the diagram below, **—** and **+** represent the two opposite alternatives, while the **O** in the middle represents you, the observer, who can see both alternatives.)

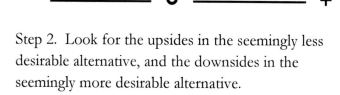

Step 2. Look for the upsides in the seemingly less desirable alternative, and the downsides in the seemingly more desirable alternative.

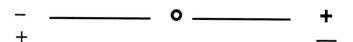

Now you can see this situation from a perspective of increased complexity.

Step 3. By doing the above, you are now able to see three different alternatives: You can see one side, or the other, or both together. A familiar example of this in the everyday world is the old question: "Is the glass half empty, or half full?" By applying the process of Balanced Thinking, you can now answer "The glass can be seen as half empty, or it can also be seen as half full—or I can see that both answers are true." In other words, Balanced Thinking allows you

81

to apply the even more complex perspective of "Both-And" Thinking.

Both-And Thinking

Both-And Thinking is a truly sophisticated way of thinking that allows us to deal with complexity more effectively. Roger Martin, the dean at the Rotman School of Management at the University of Toronto studied business executives who were able to hold two opposing ideas in their mind at the same time. His research shows that business leaders who are able to do Both-And Thinking are more effective at resolving tensions between opposing ideas and generating innovative outcomes than are executives who rely on simplistic either/or thinking.[22]

Here are some examples of how you can use Both-And Thinking in your own life.

1. "Am I weak, or am I strong?" One-dimensional Absolute Thinking can only give you one answer: Either you are weak, or you are strong. Because our False Self can only think one-dimensionally, it says that you are either weak, or you are strong, period. If you have the slightest weakness in you, then you are not strong. By contrast, Both-And Thinking allows you to realize that "Even though I have weaknesses and flaws, I am also strong." That's Both-And thinking.

2. Becoming an Empty Nester: When something troubling happens to you, Both-And Thinking allows you to find new alternatives to this apparently negative situation. For example, many people lose their sense of identity and purpose when their children grow up and leave home. Their thinking goes something like this: "My kids no longer live with me, so I've lost a key part of my identity. I am no longer their caretaker. I've lost a major source of my meaning and purpose in life. My life is in a state of upheaval because of this change. I'm not sure who I am now."

Both-And Thinking allows you to realize that—"Yes, I've lost a major source of my identity—but I can also create a new sense of identity for myself. I can find new sources of meaning and purpose in my life."

3. Losing your job: This is a major blow to anyone's life, not only for financial reasons, but also because our work is a key source of our identity and feelings of self-worth. Someone trapped in one-dimensional Absolute Thinking might respond this way: "I've lost the primary source of my identity; I've lost a central basis for purpose and self-worth in my life. My life is in a state of upheaval because of this loss."

By contrast, Both-And Thinking allows you to realize that "Yes, I've lost my job and my life is in a major state of upheaval—but I can also find a new job. And I can find other sources of meaning, purpose, and self-worth for myself while I am looking for a job."

Applying the Principle of Mutuality and Balanced Thinking in your own life

Whenever you find yourself taking a one-dimensional approach—either at work or in some other part of your life—remember that there is always an opposite alternative to what seems like the only way. And if you are faced with two opposite choices—and if one of them seems better than the other—remember that even the seemingly positive alternative can have downsides, while the seemingly less desirable alternative can have upsides.

The Principle of Mutuality helps you develop a Both-And perspective. This awareness enables you to make more robust decisions about yourself, because you now understand that you have both strengths and weaknesses. This more balanced approach can also help you identify new alternatives about who you are and what you want to do, that you may not previously have been aware of.

As the Principle of Mutuality expands your perceptions, it can markedly improve both your effectiveness and the quality of your life. It can help you move from a narrow, rigid, limited way of thinking to a new openness and freedom in both how you think and what you do. By freeing up your mind, the Principle of Mutuality creates space for your True Self, with all its new abilities and potentials, to begin emerging.

The exercises that follow will help you further explore the Principle of Mutuality and Balanced Thinking.

Exercises for The Principle of Mutuality:

The universe is created and maintained through the dynamic balance of complementary opposites.

Application: If you have only one option, you can balance it by creating an opposite alternative to it. If one alternative appears positive and the other negative, expand your thinking by looking for the downsides in the positive aspect, and the upsides in the negative aspect; remember that every alternative has both positive and negative aspects.

Exercise 1-A. Generating opposites.

For each of the following words or phrases, think of and write down an opposite term.

up_____

night_____

hot_____

dark_____

no alternatives_____

blocked_____

relaxed_____

external_____

empty_____

positive_____

work_____

negative outcome_____

flexible_____

False Self_____

open-minded_____

impossible_____

Exercise 1-B. Positive and negative aspects of my current life.

Think about and fill in the following table:

Positive Aspects of My Life Now	Negative Aspects of My Life Now

Exercise 1-C. My strengths and weaknesses.

Because everyone has both strengths and weaknesses, think about and fill in the following chart for yourself.

My Strengths	My Weaknesses

Exercise 1-D. Positive and negative aspects of being an Extreme Perfectionist.

Reread the discussion of Perfectionism in Chapter 1. Would you consider yourself an Extreme Perfectionist?   If the answer is Yes, then think about and fill in this chart:

Positive Aspects of Being an Extreme Perfectionist	Negative Aspects of Being an Extreme Perfectionist

Promoting neuroplastic changes in your brain: The latest discoveries in brain science reveal that we can literally rewire our own brains by changing how we think or act. However, in order to accomplish this, you need to repeatedly practice the new thinking style or new behavior that you want to bring into your life. The following exercise will help you practice the Principle of Mutuality so it becomes a natural part of you.

Exercise 1-E. Practicing Balanced Thinking

From now on, whenever you have to make a choice or a decision, apply the Principle of Mutuality.

- **Expand your thinking.** Instead of automatically accepting the first choice or answer that comes into your mind, consider if there might also be an alternative choice available. Is there an opposite possibility to the first choice you thought of?

- **Look for both the positive and negative aspects on each side.** Remember that every option has both positive aspects (upsides) and negative aspects (downsides). For each alternative, think about both its upsides and downsides.

- **Notice the changes this Principle brings.** As you continue to apply the Principle of Mutuality in your life, you will discover that it helps you think more creatively and make better decisions.

SELF-DISCOVERY CHECKLIST: Steps toward your True Self	✓
1. The Principle of Mutuality. I can create dynamic balance in how I think, by moving beyond one-dimensional, All-or-Nothing thinking.	
• For any idea, I can create an opposite alternative to it, so I can now see two alternatives.	
• I can look for both the upsides and the downsides in each alternative.	
• As I envision myself standing in the middle between two opposite alternatives, I can hold the possibility of Both-And in my mind.	
• I can practice dynamic Both-And thinking.	
Comments:	

SEVEN STEPS TO CONNECT TO YOUR TRUE SELF

1. **Expanding my thinking**
2.
3.
4.
5.
6
7.

*****

Chapter 4.

Expanding Your Options:
The Principle of Association

Are you ready to expand your thinking even further, so you can increase the options and possibilities in your life?

Principle #2, the Principle of Association, introduces you to the expanded possibilities created by Multi-Valued Logic and Continuum Thinking.

2. The Principle of Association
At a deeper level, seeming opposites are connected by a continuum.

Application: This continuum represents a process with many different steps. You don't have to choose between two opposite extremes; you have many options within the "gray areas."

The polarized approach of Absolute Thinking causes you to view, interpret and explain everything in exclusively "right" or "wrong" terms and to judge yourself negatively if you have even the slightest bit of some negative quality in yourself. The Principle of Association transforms this polarized approach of Absolute Thinking. By reminding us that there is actually a continuum of possibilities between two opposite extremes, the Principle of Association helps expand the options and choices available to you, and helps you develop a more accurate perception of who you really are.

Scott B. was ready to leave the New England-based food distribution company he owned, but first he had to pass his business on to new owners and develop a plan for a satisfying new life after leaving his company. After I explained the Principle of Association to him, he realized that this transition was not a quick jump from one lifestyle to another, but involved a series of steps as he moved from being an owner into a successful new life. This continuum perspective enabled him to consider a variety of options for how to pass on his company successfully, and allowed him to create a more comprehensive and meaningful plan for the new activities he could pursue in his new life.

The Principle of Association is based on the fact that not only are all aspects of the universe created by dynamic balance between complementary opposites, but in fact, at a deeper level, seeming opposites are actually connected by a continuum.

The color spectrum is an example of a continuum. When white light is passed through a prism, an entire continuum of colors appears— flowing from violet and indigo to blue, green, yellow, orange, and red.

The Principle of Association is expressed by a new multi–valued logic, which teaches that what was previously believed to be a void between two separate, polarized opposites is actually a continuum connecting each pair of opposites. This continuum is filled with numerous partial steps between the two end points—numerous degrees of interplay between the two opposites.

Mathematicians have recently developed new logic systems called "many-valued logics" (also known as "multi-valued logics"), based on the premise that rather than being disconnected, opposites are actually complementary and connected by a continuum. For example, in the 1920s, Polish logician Jan Lukasiewicz developed a new system of many-valued logic by adding a new category to the classical Aristotelian logic system.[23] According to the Aristotelian either/or logic, if statement (1) is true, then its opposite (0) becomes false. But if statement (1) is false, then its opposite, (0) must be true. (See Figure 4.)

Figure 4. The Aristotelian Logic System

STATEMENT	NEGATION
1	0
0	1

Lukasiewicz broadened the either/or paradigm by adding a third value: a half. (See Figure 5.)

Figure 5. Lukasiewicz's Many-Valued Logic System of the Included Middle

STATEMENT	NEGATION
1	0

0---- 0.5 ----1

$\frac{1}{2}$

The implications of Lukasiewicz' invention are revolutionary. Adding a third number— 0.5 — demonstrates that we can break out of a polarized perspective that says we can have only two opposite options (such as either "all-Black" or "all-White"), and instead we can move to a continuum way of thinking that enables you to recognize and interact with numerous "gray" areas in life. This continuum perspective is expressed by an even newer many-valued logic system called "fuzzy logic." Fuzzy logic deals with values expressed as degrees of a given quantity.[24]

Fuzzy logic has numerous practical applications. Because it is based on "if/then" propositions and "more-or-less" assumptions, it is actually more precise than polarized either/or logic.

Fuzzy logic is being used to create products such as microwave ovens that watch over meals with precise care, and washing machines that with a single push of a button measure out detergent and choose the correct water temperature. In Japan, a subway system run by fuzzy logic is so smooth that when the train stops or starts, you don't even have to hold on to a strap. I was fascinated as I learned about this new multi-valued logic and thought about its broader implications. I realized that becoming aware of a continuum between two opposites could transform my view of myself and my life even further. This inspired me to develop the second principle in the System for Self-Discovery: the Principle of Association.

The Principle of Association helps you realize that the continuum between opposites also represents the numerous options from which you can choose in all aspects of your own life. The many points on the continuum represent the numerous options generated by Balanced Thinking, rather than the All-or-Nothing perspective of Absolute Thinking. By providing you with more information, the Continuum Thinking of the Principle of Association can stretch your mind to new possibilities, which is essential for thinking more effectively and living more successfully.

The following diagram can help you visualize and apply the Principle of Association. (See Figure 6.)

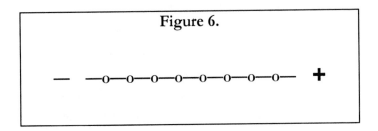

Figure 6.

Note that in this diagram, the two opposite ends are connected by a continuum which contains many different gradations between them. For example, if these two opposite end points are "black" and "white," this continuum represents the many varying shades of gray between the two end points of black and white.

There are actually two different types of continuums—"Proportional Continuums" and "Process Continuums."

A Proportional Continuum is a series of sequential proportions **between two mathematical end points.** For example, if the two end points are 0% and 100%, the continuum between them would contain numerous possible values such as 10%, 20%, 30%, etc. If the two end points are an empty glass and a full glass, the continuum between them would contain numerous possibilities such as "the glass is one-quarter full," "the glass is half full," "the glass is three-quarters full," etc.

A Process Continuum represents *a series of steps over time.* For example, if the two end points of the process are "entering high school (or college)" and "graduating from high school (or college)," the continuum between them would contain numerous steps, such as "freshman year," "sophomore year," "junior year," and "senior year." A Process Continuum perspective is especially important when you are making a transition in your life. If the two end points of this transition are "Having a full-time job" and "Retiring," the continuum between them would contain the many steps needed to design, plan, and implement a successful new life after retirement.

In contrast to a polarized approach, a continuum approach provides you with a multi-dimensional perspective that can help you become aware of new possibilities in yourself and for your life. Because the Principle of Association helps you acknowledge and deal more effectively with the "gray" areas, ambiguity and paradoxes of life, it helps you appreciate the numerous "what if's" of reality rather than the All-or-Nothing options of Absolute Thinking.

While a polarized either/or approach causes you to look for simplistic answers to complex questions, a continuum approach helps you feel more comfortable with complexity. The expanded perspectives generated by the Principle of Association allow you to develop an even more accurate understanding of who you really are, and help you increase your options and choices in life.

The following exercises will help you explore the Principle of Association and Continuum Thinking.

Exercises for Principle # 2—The Principle of Association:

At a deeper level, seeming opposites are connected by a continuum.

> **Application**: You don't have to choose between two opposite extremes; you have many options within the "gray areas."

Exercise 2-A. Exploring the "gray areas."

For each pair of opposites below, add as many words or phrases as you can think of, that fill in the "gray area" between the two opposite end-points.

Example:

Past_____**Future**
Last week *Yesterday* *Now,* *Tomorrow* *Next week*
Last year *Last month* *Next month* *Next year*

Hot_____Cold

Night_____Day

Empty_____Full

Starting_____Completing
                    a project
Birth_____Death

Exercise 2-B. Becoming aware of the continuum as a process over time.

Think of an important goal you've accomplished. Achieving this goal didn't happen overnight. Think about and write down the steps you went through in order to achieve this goal.

A **goal** I achieved:
The steps I went through in order to accomplish this goal:

Promoting neuroplastic changes in your brain:
The latest discoveries in brain science reveal that we can literally rewire our own brains by changing how we think or act. However, in order to accomplish this, you need to repeatedly practice the new thinking style or new behavior that you want to bring into your life. The following exercise will help you practice the Principle of Association so it becomes a natural part of you.

Exercise 2-C. Discovering and enjoying the "gray areas."

In the future, whenever you have a goal or project that you have to accomplish, take some time to brainstorm alternate ways of achieving this goal. Make this a fun exercise! Since the options you come up with begin in your imagination, feel free to imagine even the most fanciful or ludicrous ways of achieving your goal. Try to come up with as many possible alternatives as you can.

SELF-DISCOVERY CHECKLIST: Steps toward your True Self	✓
1. The Principle of Mutuality. I can create dynamic balance in how I think, by moving beyond one-dimensional, All-or-Nothing thinking.	
• For any idea, I can create an opposite alternative to it, so I can now see two alternatives.	
• I can look for both the upsides and the downsides in each alternative.	
• As I envision myself standing in the middle between two opposite alternatives, I can hold the possibility of Both-And in my mind.	
• I can practice dynamic Both-And thinking.	
Comments:	
2. The Principle of Association. I can expand my thinking even further by using Continuum Thinking.	

SELF-DISCOVERY CHECKLIST: Steps toward your True Self *(continued)*	✓
• I can construct a mental continuum, and see the many "gray areas" between two opposite end points.	
• Instead of assuming that I have only two choices, I can see that there are many options and possibilities available to me.	
Comments:	

SEVEN STEPS TO CONNECT TO YOUR TRUE SELF

1. **Expanding my thinking**
2. **Expanding my options**
3.
4.
5.
6.
7.

*****

Chapter 5

Connecting to Your Original Inner Core: The Principle of Centeredness

Are you ready to connect to your own original Inner Core?

Principle #3, the Principle of Centeredness, introduces you to the concept and practice of centering, which strengthens your connection to your innate authentic self.

3. The Principle of Centeredness
Each of us has an original core, or Center of Balance, which is the key to our authentic self.

Application: Through centering, you can connect to the innate wisdom of your own inner core.

Unfortunately, life's many distractions can cause us to lose touch with our True Self.

- Other people's demands on our time and energy can pull our focus away from our inner self.
- Trying to live up to external criteria can distract us from staying connected to our True Self.

105

- While on the one hand, being able to expand your thinking allows you to discover many more options in life, having too many new options and possibilities to choose from can also be overwhelming.

We need a way to stay connected to our inner core in the midst of these many distractions, and centering can provide this.

Centering also helps undo the faulty beliefs and behaviors we learned over the years, which caused us to become disconnected from our own original inner core. The real you has always been within you. Each of us was born with an original core, but we became disconnected from it as a result of the experiences and limiting beliefs we encountered throughout our lives. The Principle of Centeredness helps you slow down, listen to yourself, and connect to who you really are, so you can recognize what is truly important to you and can make the best choices for an authentic life.

Fred and Joan C., the married co-owners of a suburban golf course, were considering selling their property so they could retire. Joan continually opposed deals with potential buyers, however, because she was secretly afraid that once they retired, Fred would spend all his time golfing in their retirement community, and she would become a bored, lonely "golf widow." My work with Fred and Joan focused on the Principle of Centeredness, which helped them discover what values they shared in common. This allowed them to develop a mutually satisfactory plan for activities they would do together; with this in place, they sold their business to a new owner and went on to a fulfilling retirement.

Another couple I worked with, Ben and Stephanie D., became "empty nesters" in their early 50s, when their youngest child left home for college. This made them vulnerable to the exploding problem of "Gray Divorce"—empty nesters who separate because they can't deal with this major change in their lives. The Principle of Centeredness allowed Stephanie and Ben to discover what core values they shared, which enabled them to build a solid foundation for their dramatically altered new lifestyle.

The scientific basis for the Principle of Centeredness

You are unique. Your genetic code is unique. Your body is made up of seven billion- billion-billion atoms, but their configuration is also unique, since there is only one of you. Physically, your thumb print, eye pattern and the way you walk are all unique to you. No one like you has ever lived, or will ever live, since you are an absolutely one-of-a-kind creation—a fact which is expressed in your unique talents, the distinctive way you have put your life together and your personal history.

Our lives are full of distractions and our culture encourages us to focus exclusively on the external world around us. We learn to compare ourselves to others and judge ourselves by others' reactions to us. Instead of staying in touch with our own uniqueness, it's easy to lose ourselves in the external world, and in other people's demands and values.

Recent discoveries in brain science have revealed that we have the innate capacity to reconnect to our original inner core, through the activity of "centering." Researchers have discovered a variety of methods through which we can reconnect to our inner core. Many of these centering methods have traditionally been described as "meditation," but research has now proven conclusively that meditation or centering has a scientific basis. This is because the practice of centering actually creates physiological changes in our brain and nervous system, which allows us to think, feel, and act differently.

Researchers have documented numerous benefits from the regular practice of centering. They've found that centering helps mobilize your body's inner resources, helps heal physical and emotional diseases, induces greater relaxation, and helps reduce depression, irritability, and stress disorders. These meditative or centering practices also improve our effectiveness and success in school and at work, and by creating more inner calmness, help us improve our relationships with other people.[25] In a surprising example, at Norwich University, the oldest private military academy in the U.S., researchers found that meditation improved critical thinking and mental resilience.[26] The U.S. military has even begun using meditative techniques to improve troop performance and reduce stress, anxiety, and depression.[27]

One of the most well-known centering techniques is to focus on paying attention to your breathing, or to mentally repeat a word you have chosen, while allowing any thoughts that enter your mind to simply drift away. Scientists have documented that doing this on a regular basis, such as for 20 minutes each day, is all it takes to generate these amazing mind-body shifts inside of you. (Exercise 3-A at the end of this chapter provides more instructions for how you can explore this technique.)

In the creation of any friendship, you need to spend time with the other person. Likewise, by taking the time to center yourself—preferably on a daily basis—you can begin to restore a direct, intimate relationship with your own original core. From my own personal experience with centering, I found that the more you reconnect your life with your center on a daily basis, the better able you are to live a joyful and meaningful life.

The more I practiced centering, the more I became able to experience the wonder of life and the joy of living. Watching the natural joy of children or animals playing reawakened my own sense of joy. I began to experience joy simply by having another day of life, another opportunity to participate in life's creative play. I began to feel joy just being able to see the sun rise each morning, and knowing that I was privileged simply to be here.

Why we lose touch with our original inner core

It's important for you to remember that who you really are never left you; you simply got into the habit of not being aware of its existence deep inside you. Your inner core has been trying to connect with you over the years, as expressed by your desire to become the person you know you can be. Also, feelings of inner emptiness are another way your center has been trying to tell you that it was missing in your life.

During my journey to my True Self, I discovered how I became disconnected from my original inner core. In order to not be abandoned by my parents as a young child, I disconnected from my own inner core. My survival instincts told me that I needed to abandon my natural state of being in order to get what I needed so I could live.

I was brought up in a family where love was conditional. The message I got from my parents was: "If you do what we want, we will show love. "If not, we will withhold our love. " I learned early on that simply being myself was not "OK," and in order to be "OK" I had to perform, or act, only in certain narrow ways to be loved by my parents.

Being brought up in a family where love was conditional causes us to like ourselves only when we have accomplished something. Conditional love can create a sense of uncertainty and insecurity in us, causing us to believe that performance and external approval are the only true validations of our personal worth.

If one or both of your parents were excessively critical or demanding, or if you were brought up in a family that expected you to be 100% perfect all the time, this most likely eroded your self-confidence and caused you to doubt your own abilities.

From my own experience, I know that continually being told that something was wrong with me caused me to feel inferior, inadequate, incapable and insecure. These feelings became part of who I was. I developed ongoing self-doubt; I doubted myself, doubted what I had to offer, doubted my value, my goodness, and my ability to love. All of these contributed to my disconnection from my original inner core. Whenever the time came for me to do something that I wanted to accomplish, instead of feeling self-confident, I hesitated and became tentative and indecisive. I would often vacillate between other people's ideas. Because I doubted myself and my abilities, I often simply gave up trying.

As a result, I unknowingly turned away from the person that I was naturally meant to be. This unnatural severance from who I really was resulted in the lifelong pain of being disconnected from my True Self, which caused me to experience a general state of emptiness, sadness and unhappiness over the years.

At some point during my quest for my True Self, I realized that a good way to rediscover who I really was, was to become aware of my innate characteristics as a newborn infant. When you were a baby you were:

- Pure awareness
- Filled with potential
- Loving
- Genuine
- Full of joy and the wonder of life
- Playful
- Creative
- Bursting with unique gifts and talents

These characteristics were our natural state before we became disconnected from our True Selves.

The Experience of Centering

When I decided to practice centering, I chose a centering technique and began to practice it for 20 minutes each day. (Two simple centering techniques are described in the Exercises section of this chapter.) At first I didn't feel I was "getting it." Either my mind continued to chatter while I tried to center, or I became very drowsy. (I later learned that these experiences are common to many people when they first try to center.) I was determined to master this experience. My major distraction was that I kept wondering when the 20 minutes was going to be up, so I set a timer for 20 minutes each time I practiced. After about a month, I was able to clear my mind, the sleepiness went away, and I began to feel present in the moment. I was getting it!

My daily centering practice slowly began to affect the rest of my life, helping me feel more grounded and aware throughout the day. After I had been centering for 20 minutes every day for a few months, I began to slack off due to time constraints. Sometimes I did not have the 20 minutes to just sit down quietly and center. On those days, I felt off balance, less calm, and more easily agitated. This proved to me that centering really was having an effect, so I made a commitment to myself to center every day from then on.

Gradually the practice of centering reached out to transform more and more of my life. Each time I emerged from my 20 minutes of centering, I began to get a sense of being in touch with my original inner being—I could somehow feel that I was innately a good person, worthy of love and able to love others.

As I continued to practice centering, the constant negative mental chatter of self-deprecation and self-judgments inside my head finally stopped. I become aware of my true strengths and weaknesses, which helped me make better decisions about my life. Becoming centered also helped transform my volatile temperament. I used to live on an emotional roller coaster ride, always feeling extremes of being either really up or really down. As I became more centered, I developed an even temperament for the first time in my life. I stopped over-reacting to people, was able to find something funny in stressful situations, and realized that some things are simply not worth getting upset over.

How Centering helps you reconnect to your True Self

Centering puts you in touch with a calm, inner center of balance in the midst of life's external turmoil, and allows your mind to expand, so it becomes more aware of the world outside you, and also more open to the many hidden gifts and strengths within you.

The Principle of Centeredness encouraged me to look inward and focus my awareness on my inner self, which allowed me to really know myself. It helped me slow down and take time to become aware of what I truly valued.

Centering helped me realize that I am more than my job, more than what I own, more than who I know, since my center is the deepest part of who I am—that special space inside of me, the better part of me that was waiting to be discovered and lived. The Principle of Centeredness helped me rediscover the characteristics of who I really am, including my full potential, unique talents and gifts, and my life's purpose.

Re-grounding my life in my original inner core provided me with greater psychological stability. The more I centered my time and energy on who I really was, the more the "smoke and mirrors" created by my façade went away. And the more I became real to myself, the less I needed to hide behind a façade. My healthy ego emerged, which allowed me to take care of my legitimate needs and become more open and transparent to other people. Rather than living a life of lies, I was able to live with authenticity.

Once I began to experience my original center, I developed a heartfelt, genuine approach to life. My natural curiosity was unleashed. I also increasingly wanted to rid myself of the unnecessary mental and emotional "baggage" I had been carrying around, deluding myself that it would somehow make me happy. I realized that my entire life had been spent chasing things, while totally forgetting who I really was.

As I became more real to myself, I was able to stop always trying to please others and justifying my life to others. Centering created emotional space that allowed me to stop feeling dominated, controlled by, or inferior to, other people. I became better able to state clearly what I wanted and didn't want, and able to stand up to people who had previously been intimidating to me. Becoming increasingly centered in my True Self allowed me to maintain my psychological center and prevented me from being thrown off balance by circumstances or situations that I encountered.

Centering also helped me discover and feel good about expressing the positive "Power of No." Being able to say No to myself was one of the most empowering things I could do, because it made it possible for me to stop doing things that would be harmful in the long run. It also allowed me to be able to say No to other people who wanted their neediness satisfied at my expense. I became increasingly able to establish healthy boundaries, which allowed my newly developing True Self to grow and flourish.

Centering has helped me stay in touch with what is truly important, and with who I really am. However, I know that life is dynamic. Some days I feel more connected to my inner core and other days I feel disconnected; some days I feel really good about myself, and others I don't. The big difference is that now when I am "off center," I am not far from my original core, and I know what to do to bring myself back.

The following exercises will help you experience centering and strengthen your connection to your original inner core.

Exercises for Principle # 3—The Principle of Centeredness:

Each of us has an original core, or Center of Balance, which is the key to our authentic self.

Application: Through centering, you can connect to the innate wisdom of your own inner core.

117

Exercise 3-A. Practicing a Centering Meditation.

Much of your day is probably focused on the external, with no time for your inner self. You deserve to take the time to let your inner core emerge. Only by taking the time to center yourself on a daily basis can you restore a direct, intimate relationship with your own original core.

The most well-known and simplest centering technique is "Mindfulness Meditation." In Mindfulness Meditation, you find a comfortable place to sit, then you breathe naturally and focus your awareness on observing your breathing. If your mind wanders, simply bring it back to focus on your breath. If thoughts come into your mind, simply let your thoughts go. Do all this without judging yourself; simply keep focusing on your breathing. You can begin doing this for only a few minutes each day, and as you feel more comfortable with this practice, you can increase the length of time you do it. For more about how to do Mindfulness Meditation, see www.mindful.org/meditation/mindfulness-getting-started

Mindfulness Meditation is based on a Buddhist meditation practice. For those who want to practice centering without any religious associations, Dr. Herbert Benson of Harvard Medical School developed a "secular" version of centering that he calls the "Relaxation Response." To practice the

Relaxation Response, you choose a familiar word, such as "one" (or any simple word you feel comfortable with), and mentally repeat that word to yourself, while letting go of all other thoughts or distractions. For more about this method, see Herbert Benson, M.D., *The Relaxation Response*, Avon Books, 1975, or go to www.relaxationresponse.org .

Exercise 3-B. My personal values.

Being aware of what you truly value in life can help
you stay centered and in touch with your own Inner
Core.

From the following list, check which of the following
values are important to you.

__ Achievement	__ Growth
__ Accountability	__ Happiness
__ Appreciation	__ Health
__ Adventure	__ Helping other people
__ Affection	__ Helping society
__ Arts	__ Honesty
__ Caring	__ Independence
__ Challenges	__ Independent
__ Change and variety	Thinking
__ Close relationships	__ Influencing others
__ Community	__ Inner harmony
__ Commitment	__ Integrity
__ Competence	__Involvement
__ Competition	__ Knowledge
__ Cooperation	__ Leadership
__ Courage	__ Loyalty
__ Country	__ Love
__ Creativity	__ Meaning
__ Decisiveness	__ Money
__ Education/ learning	__ Openness
__ Effectiveness	__ Personal growth
__ Environment	__ Privacy
__ Fun/humor	__ Public service
__ Gratitude	__ Recognition

	Other:
__ Relationships	
__ Religion	_____
__ Reputation	_____
__ Responsibility	_____
__ Security	_____
__ Self-Respect	_____
__ Serenity	_____
__ Sophistication	
__ Spirituality	
__ Stability	
__ Time	
__ Trust	
__ Truth	

Exercise 3-B. My personal values *(continued)*

From the list on the previous page, write below which of the values you checked are the most important to you (maximum 10).

If possible, list these values in the order in which they are most important to you (starting with number 1 as most important).

1. _____

2. _____

3. _____

4. _____

5. _____

6. _____

7. _____

8. _____

9. _____

10. _____

Read over and reflect on the list you have written above. Now answer the following two questions:

What do the values you have chosen tell you about yourself?

_____

_____

_____

_____

_____

_____

How fully are you expressing these values in your life?

_____

_____

_____

_____

Exercise 3-C. The "I Am" exercise.

Many of us identify who we are with what we do, or with the roles that we have played in life. With the many competing demands on us, and trying to live up to an image of who we believe we are supposed to be, it can be difficult to know who we really are. The following exercise can help you connect more fully to the core of who you really are.

Outside of my work...

1. What do I enjoy doing?
2. What gives my life meaning?
3. What do I honor and respect myself for?
4. What do I admire about myself?
5. What do I appreciate about myself?
6. What do I like about myself?

7. What do I deserve praise for?
8. I am valuable for the following reasons:
9. What good things have other people said about me?
10. In addition to my work, what am I good at?
11. What am I really proud of myself for?
12. Why am I a good person?

Exercise 3-C. The "I Am" exercise *(continued)*

Now you are ready to write a very specific statement of how you define who you really are.

In the spaces below, clearly articulate your core conviction of who you really are. You might need to write only one sentence, or you may need to write more in order to help you go deeper in connecting to your True Self.

I am_____

I am_____

I am_____

I am_____

I am_____

I am_____

I am_____

Promoting neuroplastic changes in your brain:
The latest discoveries in brain science reveal that we can literally rewire our own brains by changing how we think or act. However, in order to accomplish this, you need to repeatedly practice the new thinking style or new behavior that you want to bring into your life. The following exercises will help you practice the Principle of Centeredness so it becomes a natural part of you.

Exercise 3-D. Take time to center yourself each day, anywhere, anytime.

After you have practiced centering on a regular basis, you can quickly center yourself any time when you feel the need to step back from a stressful situation or become calm. Here are a few simple techniques I use to center myself quickly:

- Imagine a line which runs up and down through the middle of your body, and focus your awareness on this centering line.

- Visualize a circle, which represents the world around you, and visualize yourself centered in the middle of that circle.

- Choose a small special object, such as a stone or bead, which you can carry in your pocket. Every time you feel this object, let it remind you of your inner core.

Exercise 3-E. Living my values.

You can use the list of your personal values from Exercise 3-B, to refer to in the days, weeks, even years to come.

If something you are doing (or something you are asked to do) does not feel right to you, you can ask yourself:

- **Does this activity reflect my values?** If not, then consider:
- **What changes can I make so I am able to live my values in this situation?**

Exercise 3-F. Remembering who you really are.

Life brings many changes and surprises. Connecting to the core self that you described in Exercise 3-C can help you stay centered and grounded in the midst of change. Take some time each day to read over this description of who you really are.

Your awareness of who you truly are can also change. If at some future time you develop a different sense of who you really are, feel free to change or add to your "I AM" description.

SELF-DISCOVERY CHECKLIST: Steps toward your True Self	✓
1. The Principle of Mutuality. I can create dynamic balance in how I think, by moving beyond one-dimensional, All-or-Nothing thinking.	
• For any idea, I can create an opposite alternative to it, so I can now see two alternatives.	
• I can look for both the upsides and the downsides in each alternative.	
• As I envision myself standing in the middle between two opposite alternatives, I can hold the possibility of Both-And in my mind.	
• I can practice dynamic Both-And thinking.	
Comments:	
2. The Principle of Association. I can expand my thinking even further by using Continuum Thinking.	
• I can construct a mental continuum, and see the many "gray areas" between two opposite end points.	✓

SELF-DISCOVERY CHECKLIST: Steps toward your True Self *(continued)*	
• Instead of assuming that I have only two choices, I can see that there are many options and possibilities available to me.	
Comments:	
3. The Principle of Centeredness. I can connect to my original inner core through the practice of centering.	
• I can find a centering practice that feels right for me, and I can practice it regularly (for at least 20 minutes each day).	
• I can observe how my life changes with my regular practice of centering.	
Comments:	

SEVEN STEPS TO CONNECT TO YOUR TRUE SELF

1. Expanding my thinking
2. Expanding my options
3. Being able to center myself
4.
5.
6.
7.

*****

Chapter 6

Reclaiming Missing Parts of Yourself: The Principle of Wholeness

---

Are you ready to explore and integrate imbalanced or missing aspects of yourself?

Principle #4, the Principle of Wholeness, helps you strengthen your True Self by showing you how to become more whole.

---

4. The Principle of Wholeness
The universe is a coherent whole, made up of countless integrated, coherent wholes.

Application: You become whole when you honor and integrate all parts of yourself—positive and negative, inner and outer, mind and body, head and heart.

Our False Self overemphasizes a few very specific parts of ourselves—in particular, our work, our ability to accomplish things, and our external successes—while downplaying or ignoring other crucial parts of our life, such as home and family life, loving relationships, and our inner emotional life, thus preventing us from being whole.

To be whole means several things: First, we must honor and value all aspects of ourselves. Second, we need to integrate parts of ourselves that have become disconnected from each other. And third, we need to recognize and reintegrate into ourselves parts that for various reasons we have repressed, ignored, or denied. The Principle of Wholeness allows us to reconnect to and reclaim all these parts of ourselves.

A familiar description of a whole individual recognizes six major areas of life—physical, emotional, social, intellectual, professional, and spiritual. When I was living from my False Self, I was aware of and living in only two of these areas—the professional and the intellectual. As I reconnected to my True Self, I began to pay attention to and spend time in all six areas of life. I began to take more care of my physical body. I became aware of my emotional life. I developed more fulfilling and loving relationships, and my life became infused with a spiritual perspective as I recognized my connection to something larger than myself and expressed my interconnectedness by giving back to my community.

The scientific basis for the Principle of Wholeness: From hierarchies to holarchies

In the Mechanistic Paradigm, the universe and everything in it is shaped by hierarchical relationships. However, the latest scientific discoveries are showing us that reality is actually shaped by "holarchies"— relationships in which the interactions between the parts and the whole are based not on power and control, not on superiority and inferiority, but instead on increasing degrees of complexity. In a holarchy, each level of reality is "nested" inside the next— higher and more complex—level. Systems of holarchies create the wholeness of nature and the nature of wholeness.[28]

Holarchies are an essential aspect of you and your life. An example is the relationship between the atoms, molecules, cells, and organ systems that make up your body. Your body is made up of atoms, which combine to create molecules, which make up the cells which comprise the tissues and organs that make up the various organ systems of your body, such as your nervous, skeletal, muscular, cardiovascular, respiratory, gastrointestinal, and reproductive systems.

At the social level, you are part of a family, a community that is part of a region, and a nation that is a member of the world community. You are also a part of the human species that exists within an ecological community, which makes up the Earth, which is part of the Solar system, which is part of the Milky Way galaxy, which is part of the Local Cluster of galaxies, which is part of the universe. Each of these entities or levels is whole unto itself, but each also joins with others of its type to create larger wholes.

Applying the Principle of Wholeness in your life

Wholeness has many meanings for us as human beings. On the one hand, it refers to integrating opposites within ourself, such as reason and emotion, or head and heart. But we are made up of more than just opposites. We are also made of distinct parts that together constitute a whole system. For example, your body is made up of many different organs and organ systems. When each of these systems is healthy and all of them are working together to ensure your health, you can say that you are whole.

One example of how to express the Principle of Wholeness in your life is by more fully using and integrating both sides of your brain. Scientists now understand that the two hemispheres of our brains each direct a different set of functional abilities. The left half of our brain is more efficient at generating abilities involving logic, language, and taking action, while the right half of our brain is more adept in the areas of music, art, and spatial relationships. Left-brain functions operate in a linear fashion, moving from cause to effect and enabling us to break down information into separate bits that we can analyze piece by piece, while the right half of our brain synthesizes material simultaneously and sees whole patterns. The right half of our brain also has special links to producing and interpreting emotions.[29]

Although each of the brain's hemispheres has its own distinct types of functions, the two halves of our brain are connected by a dense bridge of nerve fibers called the corpus callosum, which allows the two halves to communicate with each other.[30]

Western culture has a long tradition of separating our left brain from our right brain, and overemphasizing left-brain functions. While scientists recognize that certain types of tasks and thinking tend to be more associated with specific brain hemispheres, the fact is that no one is fully "right-brained" or "left-brained," and we tend to do better at tasks in which the entire brain is utilized. In order to be whole, we need to honor and value both sides of our brain, and we also need to integrate the two halves—for example, by using both our analytical and intuitive abilities, and by combining reason with emotional awareness.[31]

Our culture overemphasizes mind over body, head (reason or logic) over heart, masculine over feminine, and material, external reality over inner awareness. In these and many other ways our culture

135

teaches us to split ourselves in two, to value some parts of ourselves and devalue or even deny other parts. The belief that we are made up of pairs of disconnected opposites—one pole superior, the other inferior—also prevents us from becoming whole. In order to become whole, we need to strengthen or rebuild the devalued or repressed sides of ourselves, then integrate both sides by recognizing their connections.

It takes courage to admit that your life is unbalanced, especially if it is overly one-sided in the direction of your work activities. And it takes courage to pay more attention to devalued parts of yourself, and to bring devalued activities more fully into your life. By giving you the vision and strength to reconnect to and express all of yourself, the Principle of Wholeness can help you more fully connect to and live from your True Self.

The following exercises will help you discover missing aspects of your life, and can help you begin the process of bringing greater balance, integration and wholeness into your life.

Exercises for Principle # 4—The Principle of Wholeness:
The universe is a coherent whole, made up of countless integrated, coherent wholes.

Application: You become whole when you honor and integrate all parts of yourself—positive and negative, inner and outer, mind and body, head and heart.

Exercise 4-A. Feeling whole.

Think of a time or experience when you felt truly whole. Describe it below.

_____

_____

_____

_____

_____

_____

If possible, explain what about this experience caused you to feel whole:

_____

_____

_____

_____

_____

_____

(If you liked doing this exercise, try to think of other times when you felt whole; describe them and try to explain how they caused or allowed you to feel whole.)

Exercise 4-B. Integrating opposites in your life: Work-Life balance and Work-Family balance.

One aspect of becoming whole is being able to integrate opposites in your life.

For many of us, the challenges of creating Work-Life balance and Work-Family balance represent our struggle to become more whole. In order to bring more wholeness into your life, think about and answer the following two sets of questions:

1. Is **Work-Life balance** a challenge for you? Has your work crowded out or taken over most or all other aspects of your life?

Yes_____   No_____

If Work-Life balance is a challenge for you, then ask yourself this:

- **What changes do I want to make in my work, or in the rest of my life, so that my**

work is more reasonably balanced with the rest of my life?

_____

_____

_____

_____

_____

_____

_____

_____

_____

_____

2. Is **Work-Family balance** a challenge for you? Has your work crowded out or taken over so much of your life that it is difficult for you to spend enough time—or enough meaningful time—with your family?

Yes_____   No_____

If Work-Family balance is a challenge for you, then ask yourself this:

- **What changes do I want to make in my work, or in the rest of my life, so that I am better able to spend more time—especially more meaningful time—with my family?**

_____

_____

_____

_____

_____

_____

_____

_____

_____

_____

Exercise 4-C. A pie-chart image of your whole life.

A familiar description of a whole individual depicts six major areas of life— social, emotional, spiritual, professional, intellectual, and physical —in a pie chart.

- **How fully does this image of wholeness apply to you?** (If you don't relate to the concepts of "religious" or "spiritual," you can replace that section with another area of interest, such as "leisure" or "recreational activity.")

- Which of these areas are missing from
  your life?

_____

_____

_____

_____

- Which of these areas are you
  overemphasizing?

_____

_____

_____

_____

_____

- Which of these areas do you need to
  strengthen in your life?

_____

_____

_____

Promoting neuroplastic changes in your brain:
The latest discoveries in brain science reveal that we
can literally rewire our own brains by changing how
we think or act. However, in order to accomplish
this, you need to repeatedly practice the new thinking
style or new behavior that you want to bring into
your life. The following exercise will help you

practice the Principle of Wholeness so it becomes a natural part of you.

Exercise 4-D. Continue applying the Principle of Wholeness in your everyday life.

Refer back to the exercise above about Work-Life balance and Work-Family balance (Exercise 4-B), and the pie-chart image of your whole life (Exercise 4-C).

From your answers to these two exercises, choose an aspect or activity in your life that you want to increase. Consider how you can bring this aspect more fully into your life. Then create a plan for some changes you will make, in order to bring this aspect more fully into your life, and systematically implement your plan.

SELF-DISCOVERY CHECKLIST: Steps toward your True Self	✓
1. The Principle of Mutuality. I can create dynamic balance in how I think, by moving beyond one-dimensional, All-or-Nothing thinking.	
• For any idea, I can create an opposite alternative to it, so I can now see two alternatives.	
• I can look for both the upsides and the downsides in each alternative.	

SELF-DISCOVERY CHECKLIST: Steps toward your True Self *(continued)*	✓
• As I envision myself standing in the middle between two opposite alternatives, I can hold the possibility of Both-And in my mind.	
• I can practice dynamic Both-And thinking.	
Comments:	
2. The Principle of Association. I can expand my thinking even further by using Continuum Thinking.	
• I can construct a mental continuum, and see the many "gray areas" between two opposite end points.	
• Instead of assuming that I have only two choices, I can see that there are many options and possibilities available to me.	
Comments:	

	✓
SELF-DISCOVERY CHECKLIST: Steps toward your True Self *(continued)*	
3. The Principle of Centeredness. I can connect to my original inner core through the practice of centering.	
• I can find a centering practice that feels right for me, and I can practice it regularly (for at least 20 minutes each day).	
• I can observe how my life changes with my regular practice of centering.	
Comments:	
4. The Principle of Wholeness. I can create wholeness for myself by recognizing, strengthening, and integrating previously devalued or ignored aspects of my life.	
• I can recognize undervalued areas of my life that I need to pay more attention to.	
• I can devote time and energy to strengthening missing areas of my life.	
Comments:	

SEVEN STEPS TO CONNECT TO YOUR TRUE SELF

1. Expanding my thinking
2. Expanding my options
3. Being able to center myself
4. Becoming more whole by discovering and integrating missing aspects of my life
5.
6.
7.

*****

Chapter 7.

Exploring and Transforming Your Shadow:
The Principle of Wholeness,
(*continued*)

Are you ready to explore and transform your uncomfortable, undesirable, and painful beliefs, emotions, and memories that you have buried outside of your conscious awareness?

To help you become even more whole and more fully yourself, Principle #4, the Principle of Wholeness, also helps you acknowledge, explore, and transform the contents of your Shadow.

4. The Principle of Wholeness
The universe is a coherent whole, made up of countless integrated, coherent wholes.

Application: You become whole when you honor and integrate all parts of yourself—positive and negative, inner and outer, mind and body, head and heart.

In my journey to authenticity, I discovered that denying these negative aspects of myself was actually preventing me from fully becoming my True Self. The only way I could make real, meaningful changes in my life was to first become aware of the unconscious negative beliefs and images that I had about myself. I also needed to remember all of the negative things I had done, all of the people I had hurt, and all of the times that I had been hurt, all of which I had repressed and denied. I found that only by consciously acknowledging these long-buried negative aspects of myself could I create genuinely positive feelings about myself.

Robert E., the owner of a precision manufacturing company in the Midwest was in his mid-60s. The question of leaving his business was of increasing importance, but he evaded this topic whenever it came up. As I worked with him, he became aware of unacknowledged issues in his Shadow—especially fear of failure and fear of anticipated mental anguish when he no longer had the role of owner to fill his life. Once Robert realized how these fears were preventing him from thinking effectively about selling his company, he was able to break out of his procrastination trap, and actively developed and implemented a transition plan for his company and himself.

Many of us deny negative aspects of ourselves by burying them in a part of our unconscious mind that the eminent psychologist Carl Jung named "the Shadow." As Jung explains it, our Shadow is filled with a lifetime of uncomfortable feelings and shameful experiences, such as emotional pain we experienced but wanted to forget and all the pain we caused others that we wanted to deny.[32]

Psychologists explain that we mentally repress what becomes too painful for us to experience consciously, but these repressed feelings and memories are still inside us, part of our unconscious mind. These unconscious beliefs, feelings, and memories can still shape our lives, without us being aware of what is driving our emotional responses and actions.[33]

In my own life, I had created the façade of an inflated False Self-Image of absolute perfection and success, as overcompensation for the deeply negative beliefs about myself that I had buried in my Shadow. In psychological terms, my False Self was actually a defense against this deeply negative self-image that I carried in my unconscious mind. The irony was that neither of these two extremes was who I really was. I was not the overinflated False Self-Image of absolute perfection I had created, but neither was I this terrible person that my unconscious negative self-image told me I was.

In order to connect to my True Self, I first had to become consciously aware of the unconscious beliefs, emotions, and memories in my Shadow, so that I could integrate them into my life; only then could I transform their limiting, harmful impacts on me.

Exploring my Shadow

Before I acknowledged my Shadow, I projected my negatives outward by criticizing and blaming others for my mistakes and failures, which bolstered my own False Self with its illusions of perfection and power. When I began to acknowledge and explore my Shadow, I was astonished to discover my own fears, feelings of guilt, shame, vulnerability, and lack of self-esteem—exactly the opposites of the False Self I had created.

These negative feelings were so painful that for most of my life I had to cover them up or deny their existence. It was only when I accepted that I had these feelings, that I was released from their grip, which enabled me to create new positive alternatives for myself, leading to a healthy sense of self-love.

I discovered that my Shadow held many negative aspects of myself, including extremely limiting, closed beliefs; a fearful, anxious emotional response to life; a tendency toward self-defensive behaviors; as well as numerous negative beliefs that prevented me from having psychological essentials such as feelings of self-esteem, value, and self-worth.

I discovered that my Shadow actually consisted of two distinct parts (See Figure 7.):

- The "Top" of my Shadow contained the parts of myself and my life experiences that I had hidden from other people (and even hidden from myself), parts that I denied because these aspects didn't live up to my ideal image of myself—they didn't fit who I thought I was "supposed" to be.

- The "Bottom" of my Shadow held the many faulty, harmful, limiting, negative beliefs and painful emotions I had learned from other people, especially from my parents and teachers.

In order to connect to my True Self, I first had to become aware of and consciously transform both parts of my Shadow.

Going deeper: Transforming the Shadow

One of the most difficult aspects of connecting to my authentic self was the process of recognizing and dealing with my Shadow. During my journey of self-discovery, I began to realize that I had been so focused on always being positive, always thinking positively, that I had repressed undesirable and painful parts of myself out of my conscious awareness. I gradually began to recognize that these unconscious parts of myself actually had an enormous impact on how I felt about myself and on how I was living; in fact, these unconscious aspects were a major source of my False Self, since they made me believe that who I really was, was not good enough, and I had to create and live from a False Self-Image in order to be happy and successful.

151

Figure 7. The False Self, the Shadow, and the
True Self

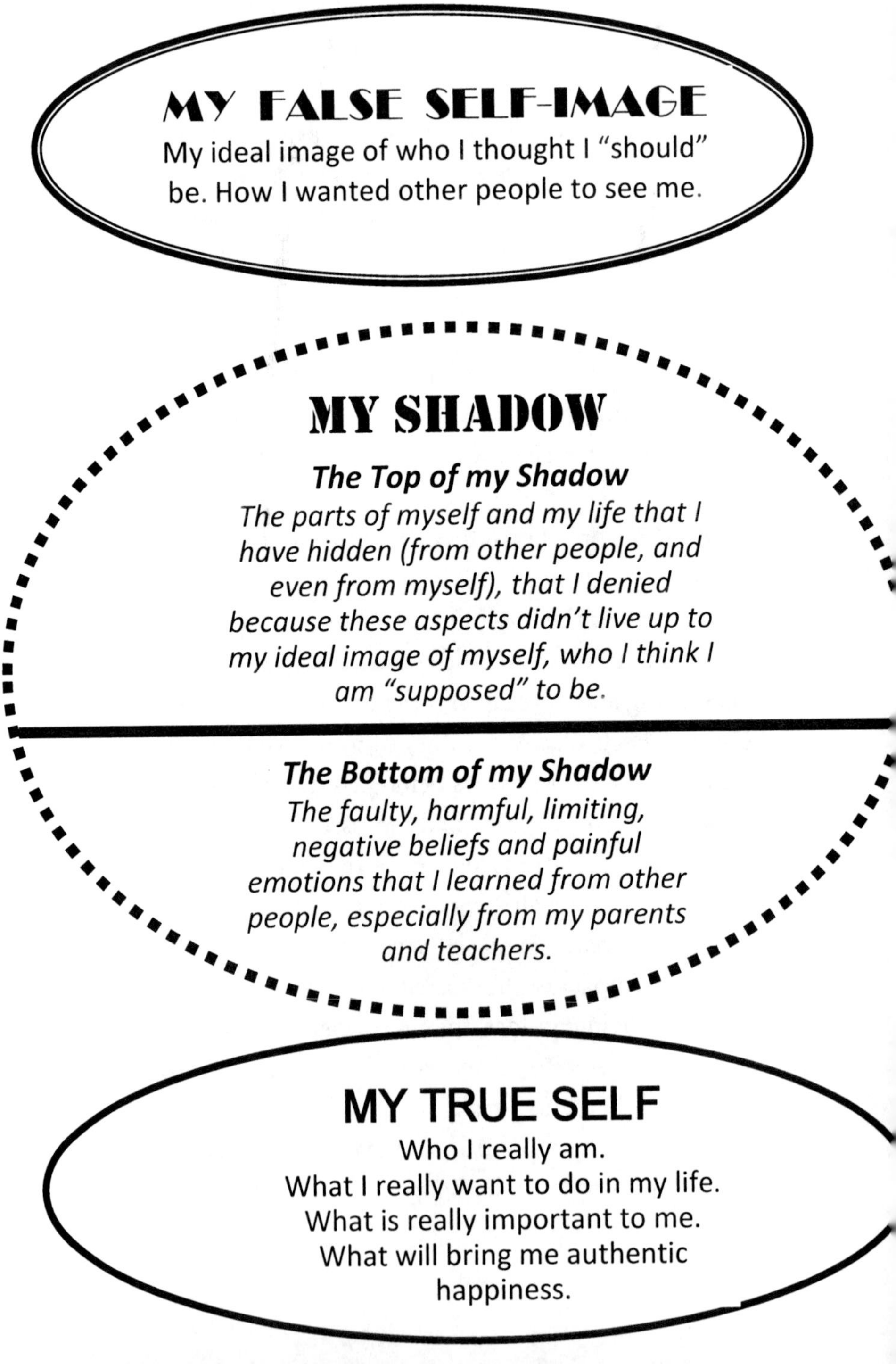

MY FALSE SELF-IMAGE

My ideal image of who I thought I "should"
be. How I wanted other people to see me.

MY SHADOW

The Top of my Shadow

*The parts of myself and my life that I
have hidden (from other people, and
even from myself), that I denied
because these aspects didn't live up to
my ideal image of myself, who I think I
am "supposed" to be.*

The Bottom of my Shadow

*The faulty, harmful, limiting,
negative beliefs and painful
emotions that I learned from other
people, especially from my parents
and teachers.*

MY TRUE SELF

Who I really am.
What I really want to do in my life.
What is really important to me.
What will bring me authentic
happiness.

I also realized that in order to connect to my True Self, I first had to recognize and acknowledge the hidden contents of my Shadow. Only then could I transform their harmful impacts on myself and my life.

Toxic Shame

Shame is a powerful emotion. In appropriate situations, a healthy sense of shame is both good and necessary. For example, feeling ashamed of yourself when you do something hurtful to someone else—or to yourself—can prevent you from doing this hurtful act again. And by not repeating this type of activity, you know that you will not have to feel ashamed of yourself in the future. By contrast, Toxic Shame is the identification with the assumption that you are innately bad and evil, the condition of feeling that you are defective, unworthy, and undeserving of love, and there is nothing you can do to change this feeling.[34]

I discovered that a major component of my Shadow consisted of deeply negative beliefs about myself caused by feelings of Toxic Shame that I carried within me. Toxic Shame refers to the feeling that you are inferior, worthless, valueless, and undeserving of happiness and success. Many of us carry feelings of Toxic Shame and faulty beliefs about our innate unworthiness, and we create a grandiose False Self-Image to overcompensate for our inner feelings of worthlessness.

Starting in early childhood (and continuing through adulthood) our feelings of Toxic Shame disconnect us from our True Self, by conditioning us into assumptions of insignificance (you're not really important), a negative self-image (you're basically no good), and negative beliefs about yourself (I really don't deserve happiness or success).

Often during my work in personal transition planning, I have seen how shame-based feelings cause people to believe that they will be unimportant, irrelevant and worthless once they leave their full-time position. And if they had low self-esteem in the past, it will be even lower when they no longer have full-time work to supply them with a sense of self-worth.

Toxic Shame was a pervasive emotion in my Shadow. Like many of us, since childhood I had taken in and believed many negative self-images and feelings about myself that told me I was inherently unworthy. My feelings of shame caused me to feel loathing toward myself.

My own hidden feelings of Toxic Shame not only made me unaware of my True Self; they also made me unaware of my unique talents and gifts. As I overcame my own feelings of Toxic Shame, I reconnected with my True Self and become aware of all the valuable things that I had to offer the world.

Being ashamed of who you are is an identity issue. Shame produces self-doubt and can cause us to experience inferiority, loneliness, and emptiness. Because Toxic Shame feels so painful, we hide these feelings in our Shadow. This makes us unaware of how much we may have identified ourselves at the core of our beings with negative assumptions about ourselves, such as I am bad, I am worthless, I am defective, I am a fraud, I am unlovable.

Although we may not be consciously aware that we are carrying around deeply negative assumptions, we live with the results of these assumptions—such as not knowing who we are, feeling low self-esteem, feeling empty and worthless, experiencing a general sense of sadness, constantly thinking negative thoughts about ourselves, criticizing and doubting ourselves, not wanting to see or hear ourselves, and avoiding looking at and disliking our bodies. When our core identity is that I am bad, worthless, defective, unlovable, we overcompensate by creating a grandiose False Self-Image.

The negative beliefs stored in my Shadow had three disempowering effects on my life. First, I constantly belittled myself; I saw myself as unimportant, and I fundamentally disliked who I was. Second, I constantly doubted myself. I would always ask myself, "Why should I try to achieve what I want in life, since I am incapable of achieving it?" Doubting myself, doubting what I had to offer, doubting my value, doubting my goodness, doubting my ability to love, all contributed to my feeling insignificant. And third, I often made self-accusatory statements to myself, blaming myself for anything that went wrong. I later realized that these self-accusatory statements were actually replays of old messages of blame and criticism I had experienced over and over again as a child. These constant messages caused me to believe that I must have been a bad person, or else my parents wouldn't have treated me this way.

The letters that spell the word "shame" reflect the impact that Toxic Shame has in our lives:

S stands for self-sabotaging patterns, often referred to as "shooting oneself in the foot," because we feel we don't really deserve to be happy or successful.

H is for the feelings of humiliation we still carry from having been humiliated when we were children.

A is for anxiety, caused by feeling that we are not being honest with ourselves.

M is for being melancholic, feeling sad, unhappy, and having a general sense of depression.

E is for being emotionally disconnected, both from ourselves and from others.

Over the years I have heard so many of my clients say that the "old tapes," the self-critical voices, old demons and old negative childhood conditioning were holding them back from transitioning into a satisfying new life. Using the System for Self-Discovery to explore and transform their Shadow, they were able to break free from these old tapes, and were able to replace their inner sense of low self-esteem with a new, healthy sense of self-importance as they began to reconnect to their True Self.

Where did our feelings of Toxic Shame come from?

These beliefs and feelings of Toxic Shame are created in us as we experience and take in the qualities and mindsets of our caretakers—from our parents, grandparents, other relatives and mentors—during infancy and childhood. Their values and judgments of us contributed to forming our concept of ourselves. If our caretakers felt weak and insecure, we as infants observed and learned from these feelings.

In my own life, I learned to believe that I was inherently defective. For example, if as a child I spilled milk or broke a dish, my parent's response was "What's wrong with you? Why can't you watch what you're doing?" I internalized this critical voice, accepted that I was guilty and shameful, and held such judgments against myself even as an adult. Since my parents valued what the neighbors thought more than they valued what I felt and who I was, I learned that I was inherently valueless.

As infants and children, we do not question what the adults in our lives are teaching us, but instead we automatically incorporate the beliefs of our parents and other caretakers, absorbing their feelings of shame and negativity, just as they had absorbed these same beliefs from their caretakers. If this was our experience, then we may grow up feeling incapable of goodness and love, which reinforces destructive behavior patterns in us later in life. Our early beliefs and convictions about ourselves become the basis on which we build our adult lives.

Our childhood experiences often caused us to disconnect from parts of ourselves that were not appreciated by our caretakers. Many of us were taught to repress emotions and behaviors that our parents considered negative. For example, you may have been told, "I never want to hear you say that again," or "We don't act like that in this family." My religious background also contributed to the creation of my Shadow, because it taught me to believe that I was sinful if I had "bad" thoughts, whether or not I acted on them.

It can be difficult to know what you really want, when you learned to be a "pleaser." As a child, I learned that my very survival depended on meeting the needs of my adult caregivers (rather than the other way around). Whenever I tried to assert my genuine needs or feelings, I was punished psychologically or even physically. Over time I lost touch with my own needs, learning that only the other person's needs were important.

Not only were we taught to repress the unacceptable parts of ourselves; we were also trained not to appreciate our innate talents. As I worked on recognizing and transforming the contents of my Shadow, I not only discovered repressed negative aspects of myself; I also became aware of natural talents that I had repressed for many years.

• Learning low self-esteem

As a child I naturally pushed to have my needs met, but I soon learned this was dangerous. In my childhood, love was given conditionally, dependent on my meeting the "security needs" of the adults around me. In order to survive as a child, I was wise to understand that I had to repress those feelings and needs which upset my parents. But the cost of self-repression was high.

Infants who receive affirming acceptance from their adult caregivers develop a firm, positive sense of self and go on to appreciate and value both themselves and others. Being demeaned and punished when we naturally seek to express ourselves and have our needs met, fosters feelings of low self-esteem which may last into adulthood, and which limit our ability to do what we truly want or need to do.

- **Overcompensating for a negative self-image**

Our definitions of success influence our attitudes and behaviors, and what we value in life. Many of us were brought up to believe that success meant the externals of status, possessions, and power—a view that negates the value of our inner self. As I continued to work on my Shadow, I began to realize that my driving need for high achievement was a reaction to having been disconnected from my original needs and my true identity. I needed to achieve external success in order to feel important and valuable. The positive feelings I gained from achievement never lasted long, because these feelings were not connected to anything positive inside myself.

Before I acknowledged my Shadow, I used to project my buried negative aspects outward by criticizing and blaming others. This bolstered my False Self, with its illusions of perfection and power. When I began to acknowledge and explore my Shadow, I was astonished to discover fear, guilt, shame, vulnerability, neediness, and lack of self-esteem within myself—exactly the opposites of the False Self I had created. These feelings were so painful that for most of my life I denied them and overcompensated for them through the overblown illusions of my False Self. Only when I accepted that I truly had these feelings, was I released from their grip.

Transforming My Shadow: Awareness, Acceptance, and Action

In order to transform the impact my Shadow had over my life, I used a three-step process of Awareness, Acceptance, and Action.

- **Step 1. Awareness**

I became aware that I had a Shadow inside myself and the unrecognized beliefs, emotions, experiences and memories in my Shadow had a powerful influence over my life, and were controlling me.

- **Step 2. Acceptance**

As I became aware of the contents of my Shadow, I realized I had to accept it in order to release their hold over me. Acceptance does not deny the reality of who I am, what I have done to others, and what happened to me. Instead, I learned to simply accept who I was, including any negative elements of my past—and then let them go. If I felt that other people (such as my parents) were responsible for creating these negative beliefs about myself that I carried, I also accepted that those people did the best they knew how, and it was not their intent to be malicious. They were simply acting as they were taught, in reaction to how their experiences influenced them.

Forgiving yourself is an important part of acceptance. Forgiveness cleanses our negative feelings, by allowing you to let go of your resentment and shame, and feelings of guilt or inferiority. The more you release these negative feelings, the more space you create for more positive beliefs and feelings to become part of you.

- **Step 3. Action**

As I became aware of the negative contents of my Shadow, including the ways I had hurt other people and myself over the years, I was then able to decide that I would no longer engage in these harmful or destructive actions. I now had the power to stop doing these harmful actions, and instead to act in more beneficial, supportive and constructive ways.

This change contributed to a "Virtuous Circle," which helped me feel increasingly better about myself. As I continued to act differently, I increasingly developed new, more positive beliefs about myself, because I could see and feel that I was acting in new and more positive ways. The more I engaged in positive new actions, the better I felt about myself, and the more my feelings of shame dissolved. The more my negative feelings about myself melted away, the more able I was to develop new positive feelings about myself, and the more I reconnected to my True Self.

162

Exploring my Shadow brought me numerous benefits. Most important, it helped me regain my innate wholeness. By exploring my Shadow, I was finally able to confront, rather than evade, what I most feared. Accepting what I had for so long felt was unacceptable greatly reduced the feelings of guilt, insecurity and shame buried within my unconscious. Exploring my Shadow also gave me more energy for life, since I was no longer wasting my energy in denial and repression. The sense of empowerment I began to feel as I gradually reconnected to my True Self allowed me to become tolerant, first toward myself, and then toward other people.

Through my inner journey, I realized that I needed to accept that my Shadow may never go away completely. Using the Seven Principles of the System for Self-Discovery, however, I found that I could create genuine, positive assumptions, beliefs and convictions, and a genuinely positive self-image about myself which dilutes the Shadow. As I worked on my Shadow, my overcompensating, inflated False Self gradually melted away and my healthy True Self was able to regain its natural place in my identity.

The following exercises will help you begin the process of discovering, exploring, and transforming your Shadow.

Exercises for Principle # 4—The Principle of Wholeness *(continued)*:

The universe is a coherent whole, made up of countless integrated, coherent wholes.

Application: You become whole when you honor and integrate all parts of yourself—positive and negative, inner and outer, mind and body, head and heart.

Exercise 4-F. Exercises for Exploring Your Shadow.

This exercise can help you become more aware of how the negative contents of your Shadow have influenced your life. Take time to think about and answer the following questions:

Do I have feelings of inferiority? If Yes, what do I feel inferior about?

Do I feel unworthy, bad, defective? If Yes, what are the reasons why I feel this way about myself?

What am I most afraid of in my life?

Whom have I hurt most in my life, and how?

What do I believe is the worst thing I have ever done?

Exercise 4-G. Toxic Shame Awareness List.

In order to feel that you are an innately worthwhile, good, valuable person, you need to become aware of your feelings of Toxic Shame. For the chart below, think about and list some of the hurts you've caused, things you've done, things you did not do, unpleasant events that happened to you that you have hidden over the years. Consider your hidden sources of Toxic Shame, both personally and professionally.

Personal	Professional

Promoting neuroplastic changes in your brain:
The latest discoveries in brain science reveal that we can literally rewire our own brains by changing how we think or act. However, in order to accomplish this, you need to repeatedly practice the new thinking style or new behavior that you want to bring into your life. The following exercise will help you practice the Principle of Wholeness so it becomes a natural part of you.

Exercise 4-H. Shadow-Talk Journal: What, Who, Feelings, and Triggers.

A Shadow-Talk Journal helps you bring your Shadow to light, eliminating its unconscious need to continually repeat the same negative messages. You will find that the more you use this journal to explore your Shadow and acknowledge your long-buried negative beliefs and messages, the less they will undermine your conscious efforts to become more positive and whole.

This is how the Shadow-Talk Journal works: Whenever you feel self-critical or hear yourself giving yourself a negative message (either in your mind or out loud), write the letters **WWFT** vertically down the left side of a piece of paper or in a notebook, leaving a few lines of space after each letter. Then, next to each letter, write your answer to the question it represents.

167

The first *W* stands for **What**—"**What** negative message am I giving myself?" As you become aware of and acknowledge what your Shadow is saying to you, write it down, and also say this message out loud—this gives your Shadow a conscious voice.

The second *W* stands for **Who**—"**Who** in my life does this message most sound like?" To answer this question, try to associate each negative message with a person in your life who originally gave you that message. By recognizing its source, whenever you give yourself that same message later on, you will be able to say, "Oh! There goes So-and-So's negative message, trying to run my life again." This helps you separate who you really are from the other person's message.

The letter *F* stands for "**Feelings**," as in "How does this negative message make me **feel?**" Writing down the answer to this question helps you get more in touch with your feeling state.

The letter *T* stands for "**Trigger**," that is "What specific beliefs, circumstances, or feelings have **triggered** this message?"

Use this **WWFT** question-and-answer process each time you feel self-critical or sense a negative message coming to you from inside. Bringing your Shadow to light by answering these questions increasingly allows you to make a conscious decision

168

either to continue to obey your Shadow's negative messages, or to create alternative, positive messages. As you consciously become responsible for creating new messages to live by, you will move further towards wholeness and discovery of your True Self.

Here's an example from my own life of how I used my Shadow-Talk Journal. I felt that I had said the wrong thing to someone, and felt really bad about myself. So in my Shadow-Talk Journal, beside the first *W*, I wrote down the negative message I was giving myself: "How dumb I was!" When I said this statement out loud, I could hear its critical, judgmental tone. Next to the second *W*, I wrote down that this message actually sounded like the voice of one of my parents. Next to *F*, I wrote that this message made me feel like a failure. Next to *T*, I wrote down that this message was triggered by my belief that I must never make a mistake. When I looked at what I had written down, I realized it was unreasonable to blame myself every time something went wrong, and I was then able to let this negative message go.

Shadow-Talk Journal

W: **What** negative message am I giving myself?

W: **Who** in my life does this message most sound like?

F: How does this negative message make me **feel**?

T: What specific beliefs, circumstances, or feelings have **triggered** this message in me?

	✓
SELF-DISCOVERY CHECKLIST: Steps toward your **True Self**	
1. The Principle of Mutuality. I can create dynamic balance in how I think, by moving beyond one-dimensional, All-or-Nothing thinking.	
• For any idea, I can create an opposite alternative to it, so I can now see two alternatives.	
• I can look for both the upsides and the downsides in each alternative.	
• As I envision myself standing in the middle between two opposite alternatives, I can hold the possibility of Both-And in my mind.	
• I can practice dynamic Both-And thinking.	
Comments:	
2. The Principle of Association. I can expand my thinking even further by using Continuum Thinking.	
• I can construct a mental continuum, and see the many "gray areas" between two opposite end points.	

SELF-DISCOVERY CHECKLIST: Steps toward your True Self *(continued)*	✓
• Instead of assuming that I have only two choices, I can see that there are many options and possibilities available to me.	
Comments:	
3. The Principle of Centeredness. I can connect to my original inner core through the practice of centering.	
• I can find a centering practice that feels right for me, and I can practice it regularly (for at least 20 minutes each day).	
• I can observe how my life changes with my regular practice of centering.	
Comments:	
4. The Principle of Wholeness. I can create wholeness for myself by recognizing, strengthening, and integrating previously devalued or ignored aspects of my life.	
• I can recognize undervalued areas of my life that I need to pay more attention to.	

SELF-DISCOVERY CHECKLIST: Steps toward your True Self*(continued)*	✓
• I can devote time and energy to strengthening missing areas of my life.	
• I can create even greater wholeness in my life by recognizing and transforming the contents of my Shadow.	
• I am willing to look at the faulty negative beliefs that I have about myself.	
• I am willing to acknowledge undesirable aspects of myself, and hurtful things I have done, that I tried to ignore.	
• I am willing to forgive myself for these aspects and activities.	
• I can change my behavior, so that in the future I will no longer act in these ways.	
Comments:	

SEVEN STEPS TO CONNECT TO YOUR TRUE SELF

1. Expanding my thinking
2. Expanding my options
3. Being able to center myself
4.a. Becoming more whole by discovering and integrating missing aspects of my life
4.b. Transforming faulty negative beliefs about myself by exploring my Shadow
5.
6.
7.

*****

Chapter 8

Bringing More Love into Your Life: The Principle of Love-in-Action

Are you ready to explore how your False Self and your Shadow have prevented you from bringing love fully into your life?

Principle #5, the Principle of Love-in-Action, helps you understand why you need to love yourself first, and shows you how, by creating healthy self-love, you can bring more loving relationships into your life.

5. The Principle of Love-in-Action
Love is an innate part of us; the ability to give and receive love is innate within our genes, our brain, our mind and body.

Application: Expressing love—for other people, and especially for oneself—can make you healthier, happier, and more whole.

The Principle of Love-in-Action helps you access and experience unconditional love, which gives you permission to love yourself unconditionally, and interact with yourself and others in a totally new way. It allows love to become a motivating force in your life, which helps you move from an excessively competitive, to a more compassionate, world.

Walter F., who headed a financial planning firm, derived his feelings of self-worth and relevance solely from his work, especially from the fact that people were paying him for his services. His life was focused on a never-ending series of work goals, and he did not have much else in his life outside of his work. After closing his company, he no longer had a way to measure his personal value, and he felt unsatisfied and disoriented. The Principle of Love-in-Action was a revelation to him. Instead of looking to other people for validation or trying to measure his self-worth by his external accomplishments, he began to look inward. By focusing his awareness on himself, not only did Walter begin to like himself for who he was—he actually began to love himself. His new loving self-perception resulted in his getting involved in enjoyable, rewarding new physical activities he previously never had time for, such as rowing on a beautiful local river and participating in group bicycling rides for charitable causes.

Neuroscientists have now documented that human beings are born with the innate capacity to receive love, express love, and to connect to other people through love. We feel happy and satisfied, and our brains and hormones actually change in positive, healthy ways when we are able to connect lovingly to other people. Helping other people can be especially rewarding, since it generates a physiological state called the "helper's high."

Not only do we feel good when we are able to receive and express love. Scientists have also discovered that giving to others can make you both happier and physically healthier, and that being involved in social relationships that connect you to other people literally protects and improves your health and lengthens your life.[35]

Conditional and Unconditional Love

My negative beliefs about who I was caused me to create a façade—a false front, or wall—around myself. This façade was a store window that enticed people to look, but to never come in, because if you came too close, you might see through me and discover that I was really an awful human being. Never letting anyone enter often caused me to feel alone and separated, especially at large social or business gatherings, while keeping up my endlessly positive false front consumed a tremendous amount of time and energy.

While living behind this wall, I constantly asked myself two questions: "If I don't like myself, why should you?" and "If you love me, what is wrong with you, since who I am is not really worthy of love?"

Many of us were brought up in families like mine, where love was conditional. The message from one or both parents was "If you do what I want, I will give you love. If you don't do what I want, I will withhold love and be cold and critical toward you."

Being brought up in a family where love was conditional caused us to like ourselves only when we accomplished something. It caused me to believe that performance and external approval were the only true validations of my personal worth. The message was that my inner being was not "OK" and in order to be "OK" I had to perform, or be a certain way, in order to be accepted by my parents. As a result I did what my parents wanted, because I did not want to be emotionally abandoned by them. For many of us, our first experience of love was conditional. We had to do, or not do, something to receive our parents' love. Conditional love breeds insecurity and competition for affection. Furthermore, conditional love makes it difficult for us to accept ourselves, a prerequisite to loving ourselves. Acceptance is the greatest gift that you can give to yourself and to other people.

During my inner journey, I discovered what I call "the ABC's" of what caused me to feel unlovable to both myself and others.

A was the Assumption that loving myself was wrong, since it was an act of pride.

B was the Belief that meeting the needs and expectations of others was the only way I could get positive feedback and receive love from the world around me.

C was the Conviction that I was incapable of giving love. My inability to really love myself had a negative impact on my relationships with other people, since I was looking to others to fill the emptiness that I felt within.

What I learned on my journey of self-discovery was that only when you believe that you are worthy of love can you love yourself unconditionally—and the more you experience unconditional love, the more loving connections you are able to create in your life.

Transforming a lack of love

I had never known what my own needs were, since I had learned only how to meet the needs of other people at my own expense. To break out of this pattern I first needed to discover what my own needs were, and to take my real needs seriously.

As a child, I continually heard that "You are not worth it," "You're no good," or "You'll never amount to anything." As a result, I pulled back and stopped trying to get what I really wanted. After finding out through my journey to my True Self what my neglected needs were, I then had to take responsibility for fulfilling those real needs.

179

In order to connect to your True Self, you need to learn to love yourself first—to believe that, even with your faults and weaknesses, you are still worthy of love. Before I went on this transformational journey, I never really understood why other people loved me, since I did not love myself, and when you do not love yourself, it is hard to love anyone else or let anyone else truly love you.

As you become aware of and accept all of yourself, including your Shadow, and gradually create positive alternatives to your negatives, you simultaneously become more able to love all of yourself. You realize that who you are at the deepest level is fundamentally OK, and you can try to be the best person you can be while still accepting and loving yourself as you are.

The fact is, you need a more loving self-image to live from your True Self. In order to feel worthy of love, you first need to feel that who you really are is inherently valuable and you are worthy of love. As you value yourself more, the more you will feel worthy of love, and the more a loving self-image becomes operational in your life. When your image of yourself is one of love, it solidifies your conviction that you are an exceptional human being. A strengthening feedback system develops between your new loving self-image and your ability to know who you really are. Feeling good about yourself enhances your sense of self-worth and awareness of how inherently valuable you are—all of which reinforces your sense of significance. The more you give yourself unconditional love, the more you will develop loving connections with other people.

A loving self-image brings you back to your naturally loving state when you were an infant, and provides courage for you to do what needs to be done to actualize your potential and utilize your unique talents and skills. The more empowered you feel, the better care you will take of yourself, especially by taking care of your physical body. Taking care of your body further enhances your sense of self-worth, because the more you take care of yourself, the more you value yourself. When you love someone else, you value them, and want to spend time with them. In the same way, when you love yourself, you will take the time and energy to take care of yourself.

Healthy Self-Love

A negative sense of self can be created not only through your personal experiences of fear and shame, but also through a basic cultural misunderstanding. Many of us think of self-love as undesirable. People who love themselves are assumed to be conceited or even sinful. But in fact, there is an enormous difference between selfishness and self-love. Selfishness, the tendency to be self-centered, to view everything in relation to oneself, to

181

consider only oneself and one's own interest, and to use others only for one's self–advancement, is a defense which arises from one's negative self-image and disconnection from one's true power and inner core.

Unfortunately, in our culture, if a child (or even an adult) experiences a wonderful feeling of self-importance, which includes joy in oneself and pleasure at being uniquely oneself and being alive, they are considered proud, vain, or conceited. Children are often denied deserved praise due to the mistaken belief that they will develop a "big head." An emerging core of self-love is swallowed up by an ocean of negativity and the belief that who you really are is not important.

The fact is, the more you experience healthy self-love, the more you can develop an unselfish concern for the needs of other people. At the same time, you will no longer have to base your relationships on a need for approval from other people. The Principle of Love-in-Action helps you become aware that every person has strengths and weaknesses, and your goal is to interact with each person you meet by giving them the same love and acceptance that you give yourself. You can also set limits, so that you stay in touch with your own unique mission in life, instead of being pulled off track by other people's agendas or issues.

Rebuilding your healthy pride

Having a healthy sense of pride is also essential for reconnecting to your True Self. Many of us learned that pride is a vice, an expression of vanity, mentally unhealthy or even inherently sinful. But the fact is, a healthy sense of pride is a supportive emotion that reinforces your sense of worth and self-love. For example, pride can be understood as an emotion that comes out of your own awareness that you have lived up to your values, achieved worthwhile goals, and treated other people well.

I consider self-pride to be a healthy emotion, since it reinforces your sense that you are a valuable individual. In addition, a healthy sense of pride rebuilds your self-confidence, self-esteem and self-respect, and gives you permission to be proud of your appearance and your abilities.

As I reconnected to my True Self by learning how to love myself, I became more able to love other people. I discovered that we can experience ennobling feelings of self-love by engaging in actions such as honest achievement, genuine self-discipline, and open-hearted sharing with other people. I believe that it is essential to create centered individuals who are unafraid of self-love, because people who truly love themselves have no need to tear other people down, and are more fully able to feel and express genuine love for others.

183

Creating genuine progress through love

The Principle of Love-in-Action becomes real in your life by engaging in acts of compassion. The more love and compassion you share, the more meaning you will experience, which further strengthens your ability to live from your True Self.

The myth of progress is one of the most powerful forces in the world today, because it promises us a golden age of prosperity, in which science and technology will transform the earth into a material paradise with constantly rising incomes. This image of ever-increasing material prosperity, however, has led to a one-sided emphasis on external progress at the expense of inner development. In our striving to create a material paradise, we have temporarily lost the inner meaning of progress.

Since we are all connected, the negative misuses of technology, wealth and power harm all of us. A more loving perspective can deepen our awareness so we are able to view technological advances as external manifestations of our evolving capacity to bring more love into the world. This perspective gives us the wisdom to understand that with every major technological advance, humanity must also develop a complementary inner advance to balance the potentially negative use of the new technology while sharing its benefits more widely. In

Chapter 10 we will return to the question of how you can more fully experience and express love in your life.

The exercises that follow will help you experience the Principle of Love-in-Action and apply it to your own life, so you can bring more love into your life, beginning with loving yourself more fully.

Exercises for Principle # 5—The Principle of Love-in-Action:

Love is an innate part of us; the ability to give and receive love is innate within our genes, our brain, our mind and body.

Application: Expressing love—for other people, and especially for oneself—can make you healthier, happier, and more whole.

Exercise 5-A. Feeling loved.

Think of a time or experience when you felt loved for who you really are (not just for your accomplishments). Describe it below.

_____

_____

_____

_____

_____

_____

If possible, explain what about this experience caused you to feel loved for yourself:

_____

_____

_____

_____

If you liked this exercise, then try to think of other times when you felt loved for yourself; describe them and try to explain what about each of them caused or allowed you to feel loved.)

Exercise 5-B. I am worthy of being loved.

Fill in as many of the following statements as you can

I am worthy of love because:
I am worthy of love because:
I am worthy of love because:
I am worthy of love because:
I am worthy of love because:
I am worthy of love because:
I am worthy of love because:
I am worthy of love because:
I am worthy of love because:

Exercise 5-C. Taking care of myself.

Taking care of yourself involves knowing what you want to accomplish, picturing what you want to look like, believing that you deserve it and that you can do it, and continuously visualizing and doing the required activities in actuality. To reinforce the creation of a positive new body image for yourself, you can put a picture of a body which comes closest to what you want to look like on the refrigerator.

Continually give yourself positive feedback as you move through the process of creating your new body image. For example, if one of your goals is to lose weight, congratulate yourself if you lose even one or two pounds. Acknowledging each step you achieve will further energize your positive self-image, because success breeds success.

To bring the process of taking better care of yourself into your life, think about and answer each of the following questions:

1. What do I want to accomplish for my body?

2. What do I want to look like?

3. Visualize your new body on a daily basis.

4. Believe that you deserve it and do the required activities.

Exercise 5-D. Loving myself more.

Think about and answer the following question:

- What do I need to do to feel *unconditional love* towards myself?

_____

_____

_____

_____

_____

_____

_____

_____

Exercise 5-E. Rebuilding healthy self-pride.

Fill in as many of the following statements as you can

I am proud of myself because:
I am proud of myself because:
I am proud of myself because:
I am proud of myself because:
I am proud of myself because:
I am proud of myself because:
I am proud of myself because:
I am proud of myself because:
I am proud of myself because:

Promoting neuroplastic changes in your brain:
The latest discoveries in brain science reveal that we can literally rewire our own brains by changing how we think or act. However, in order to accomplish this, you need to repeatedly practice the new thinking style or new behavior that you want to bring into your life. The following exercise will help you practice the Principle of Love-in-Action so it becomes a natural part of you.

Exercise 5-F. Reinforcing love in my life.

1. Think about people who love you, and ask each of them why they love you.

2. Write down their answers.

3. Read these answers to yourself each day. Be sure to read this list often on days when you feel like you don't love yourself.

SELF-DISCOVERY CHECKLIST: Steps toward your True Self	✓
1. The Principle of Mutuality. I can create dynamic balance in how I think, by moving beyond one-dimensional, All-or-Nothing thinking.	
• For any idea, I can create an opposite alternative to it, so I can now see two alternatives.	
• I can look for both the upsides and the downsides in each alternative.	
• As I envision myself standing in the middle between two opposite alternatives, I can hold the possibility of Both-And in my mind.	
• I can practice dynamic Both-And thinking.	
Comments:	
2. The Principle of Association. I can expand my thinking even further by using Continuum Thinking.	
• I can construct a mental continuum, and see the many "gray areas" between two opposite end points.	

SELF-DISCOVERY CHECKLIST: Steps toward your True Self *(continued)*	✓
• Instead of assuming that I have only two choices, I can see that there are many options and possibilities available to me.	
Comments:	
3. The Principle of Centeredness. I can connect to my original inner core through the practice of centering.	
• I can find a centering practice that feels right for me, and I can practice it regularly (for at least 20 minutes each day).	
• I can observe how my life changes with my regular practice of centering.	
Comments:	
4. The Principle of Wholeness. I can create wholeness for myself by recognizing, strengthening, and integrating previously devalued or ignored aspects of my life.	

SELF-DISCOVERY CHECKLIST: Steps toward your True Self *(continued)*	✓
• I can recognize undervalued areas of my life that I need to pay more attention to.	
• I can devote time and energy to strengthening missing areas of my life.	
• I can create even greater wholeness in my life by recognizing and transforming the contents of my Shadow.	
• I am willing to look at the faulty negative beliefs that I have about myself.	
• I am willing to acknowledge undesirable aspects of myself, and hurtful things I have done, that I tried to ignore.	
• I am willing to forgive myself for these aspects and activities.	
• I can change my behavior, so that in the future I will no longer act in these ways.	
Comments:	
5. The Principle of Love-in-Action. I can become more fully my True Self by expressing more love in my life, starting with love for myself.	

SELF-DISCOVERY CHECKLIST: Steps toward your True Self *(continued)*	✓
• I know that I am worthy of love.	
• I can give healthy self-love to myself.	
• I can devote more time and energy to expressing love for the people closest to me.	
Comments:	

SEVEN STEPS TO CONNECT TO YOUR TRUE SELF

1.   Expanding my thinking
2.   Expanding my options
3.   Being able to center myself
4.a. Becoming more whole by discovering and integrating missing aspects of my life
4.b. Transforming faulty negative beliefs about myself by exploring my Shadow
5.   Being able to love myself fully
6.
7.

*****

Chapter 9.

Using Your Power to Transform Negative Situations: The Principle of Dynamic Reversal

---

Are you ready to explore your power to transform a limiting past, present, and future?

Principle #6, the Principle of Dynamic Reversal, helps you stay centered in your True Self, no matter what changes the world brings, and shows you how to use the process of change to develop your authentic self more fully.

---

6. The Principle of Dynamic Reversal
The universe is a constant flow of ever-changing reality to which we can respond creatively.

Application: You can stay centered in your True Self through both the ups and downs of life; this gives you the power to transform a negative situation, by seeing its positive potential and turning it into a positive alternative.

It's a fact that both good and bad things happen in life. Either extreme can throw you off course, by disconnecting you from your True Self and throwing you back into your old limited ways of acting.

The Principle of Dynamic Reversal reminds you that you can stay in touch with your True Self no matter what, and can respond creatively from your True Self, instead of getting stuck in old limited ways of thinking. This allows you to turn seemingly negative situations into positive alternatives. The Principle of Dynamic Reversal allowed me to become free from unrealistic optimism; instead, I was able to be enthusiastic and expect positive outcomes based on the complete facts of a situation, not on wishful thinking.

Gordon G., the CEO of a medical software company, wanted to leave his position and explore an exciting new opportunity. However, he also believed that he had to be a complete winner at anything he accomplished, otherwise he would be a total failure, and this belief held him back from moving out of his secure company position and into an uncertain new lifestyle. As I worked with Gordon, we focused on the Principle of Dynamic Reversal, which helped him feel more self-confident that if any negative experiences came up in his new life, he could respond to them effectively. This allowed him to take the leap, and he left his old position and moved on to an adventurous new life.

The scientific basis for the Principle of Dynamic Reversal

The Principle of Dynamic Reversal is based on the fact that change is the only constant in the universe. Recent scientific discoveries suggest that the creation of the universe is not a one-time event, since the universe is still expanding and evolving. The history of the universe itself is the history of constant transformation.

The universe was not created instantaneously in its present form. During the first few millionths of a second, the universe was a hot, formless soup of elementary subatomic particles, quarks and leptons. As it expanded and cooled, the particles combined into protons and neutrons. Over the next half-million years, hydrogen and helium formed, setting the stage for star formation nearly a billion years later. The components of the universe have continued to develop and evolve over billions of years, and this process of creation is still taking place. The recent discoveries made possible by the Hubble space telescope have shown us the "nurseries" in which new stars are being born.[36]

The Principle of Dynamic Reversal is evident not only in the vast reaches of the universe, but also in our daily life here on earth. The ongoing ebb and flow of waves and ocean tides is an obvious illustration of this process of continual change. Dynamic Reversal is also reflected in the cyclic

199

patterns of your body. Every day your body temperature rises, then falls within a range of one or two degrees. You reach your highest temperature, as well as your highest level of alertness during the day. The downward cycle occurs at night, when your body temperature and awareness decline; they are at your lowest point when you are asleep. This up-and-down pattern of your own body is called your "circadian rhythm."

Change is a constant—in life and in our personal experience. But change of any kind is stressful, whether that change is negative or positive. And not only is change stressful; scientific research shows that being under stress literally changes us— physically, mentally, and emotionally, by activating our fight-or-flight response—which shifts us back into more limited thinking styles, limited perceptions, and limited behaviors. Since change of any kind is stressful, going through change can shift us into a more limited thinking style and limited actions, which further increases our stress and makes it difficult for us to cope with change.[37]

When a negative situation throws us back into our old limited thinking style, we can feel stuck or trapped in that negative situation and can't see a way out. This is where the Principle of Dynamic Reversal comes in. The Principle of Dynamic Reversal is not the limited "positive thinking" of the False Self. Dynamic Reversal does not deny the existence of negative situations. Dynamic Reversal acknowledges when there is a problem—and says that we can use new abilities, such as Balanced, Both-And thinking to find new, better alternatives to the current situation.

The key to Dynamic Reversal is to shift out of your limited thinking style by reconnecting to your center. This allows you to use all the abilities of your True Self. After becoming familiar with the experience of your deep inner center, you can use this experience to help you stay centered through life's surprises, whether positive or negative. The Principle of Dynamic Reversal helps you stay centered and connected to your deepest inner wisdom through the course of life's ups and downs.

Applying the Principle of Dynamic Reversal: Staying centered through life's ups and downs

Since life is characterized by constant change, I've learned that when everything is going well, we should enjoy the positive, but be aware of the ever-changing flow of life. It would be unrealistic to assume that negative experiences will never happen to you. But rather than viewing your life's circumstances and events judgmentally, it is far more productive to use everything as a lesson to drive your growth. In fact, some of our greatest lessons can evolve from "bad" experiences.

Learning how to stay calm and positive during the flow of life, and developing a balanced mental attitude gives you the ability to respond most effectively to whatever happens. The Principle of Dynamic Reversal gives you the ability to stay centered and connected to your deepest inner wisdom through the course of life's ups and downs.

A visual image of life's ups and downs is the sine wave. As it rises and falls repeatedly, the sine wave visually depicts the process of constant change, which occurs everywhere throughout the universe.

In order to create a visual image of how centering allows you to stay balanced through the course of life's constantly changing flow, I drew the sine wave in a vertical position and added a vertical line that rises straight up through the zigzags of life, as a symbolic representation of your calm inner center. (See Figure 8.) The minus-sign on one side of this image, and the plus-sign on the other represent the ever-flowing wave of life, as it runs from negative to positive experiences, back and forth. The straight line going up and down through the center of this back-and-forth wave symbolizes your True Self, which allows you to stay centered no matter in which direction life goes. You can use this image to remind you of the Principle of Dynamic Reversal.

Figure 8. A visual representation of the Principle of Dynamic Reversal

As life moves back and forth from negative to positive experiences, you can stay centered in your True Self.

The Principle of Dynamic Reversal can help you transform how you respond to the setbacks that inevitably arise in our lives. As it allows you to experience equanimity—a calmer response—rather than feeling overwhelmed by change and what you perceive as negative events, the Principle of Dynamic Reversal provides you with inner confidence, knowing that you can handle any situation that arises, since no matter what happens, you have expanded ways of thinking and many gifts, talents, and abilities you can call on to deal with these circumstances. Helping you find creative solutions to the situations and circumstances that arise in the course of life, the Principle of Dynamic Reversal can enhance your self-esteem and also make it easier for you to accept change.

Developing resilience

You can use the Principle of Dynamic Reversal to develop resilience—the flexible capacity to be able to bounce back and quickly recover from setbacks and personal discouragement. Resilience provides you with the capacity and skill to be robust under changing conditions, by helping you find and use whatever is at hand, by improvising and being ingenious.

Resilience gives you the ability to grow through stressful circumstances. It is a fact that growth occurs in response to stress. An example is that only when your muscles are systematically worked beyond their ability to respond well can they develop increased strength. Similarly, when our existing understanding of reality is too limited to handle current experiences, it takes a mismatch to force the growth process to occur.

Knowing that you are resilient develops your sense of personal confidence about the future, because you know that you have the ability to get through difficult experiences and can do things that you might never have done before. Being aware of your innate capacity for resilience also makes it easier for you to deal with future downturns, because you realize that "I have survived this, so I can deal with other difficult situations that may come up." A resilient attitude to change increases your effectiveness in dealing with the unpredictability and surprises you might encounter as you make significant changes in your life.

How the Principle of Dynamic Reversal gives you the power to transform negative situations

If we assume that a negative situation cannot change, and we are stuck in limited ways of thinking about it, we will feel trapped by this situation. The Principle of Dynamic Reversal increases your own feelings of power over your life by expanding your thinking to help you realize that there are many possible positive alternatives to a seemingly unalterable situation.

In fact, you can use the Principle of Dynamic Reversal to transform anything that is holding you back. You do not have to be limited by your past, present, or future. You can use the Principle of Dynamic Reversal:

- To transform your old negative, limiting beliefs from the past
- To expand the possibilities of your present circumstances
- To create a new future for yourself, different from your old limiting beliefs and behaviors

I discovered four distinct ways in which Dynamic Reversal operates to help you transform negative beliefs, situations, and actions into positive alternatives:

- You can use a Both-And approach.
- You can change and expand your perceptions of the situation.
- You can become aware of and change your own negative responses to a situation.
- You can use visualization to transform a negative belief or situation into a positive alternative.

• Using a Both-And approach

When faced with a negative situation, staying in touch with your True Self helps you remember that you can transform this situation into a positive alternative by using a Both-And approach. For example, the familiar saying "When life gives you lemons, make lemonade" doesn't mean that you should throw out the lemons because they are sour. It means that you can add sugar to the lemons to create a new, more enjoyable drink that has a refreshing sweet-and-sour tang. Because your new solution—the lemonade—combines the best qualities of both sweet and sour, it exemplifies expanded, Both-And thinking.

- **Changing and expanding your perceptions of the situation**

Sometimes you can transform a seemingly negative situation simply by changing how you look at it. The situation itself may not have changed, but by expanding your perception of it, you can see new possibilities in it. For example, instead of focusing on what a situation lacks, the Principle of Dynamic Reversal can help you expand your perceptions so you can discover the positive new opportunities a seemingly negative situation offers.

Maybe there's something you wanted, that you have been looking forward to for a long time, and now you learn that you will have to wait for it a little while longer. Instead of feeling impatient or frustrated because you can't have what you want right now, you can realize that "While I'm waiting for what I want to happen, this gives me time to do something else I wanted or needed to do, until this other thing happens." (This is another way of expressing the concept that "When life gives you lemons, make lemonade.")

- **Changing your own negative responses to the situation**

Sometimes our own negative responses are making a situation worse, and we need to become aware of how we are participating in creating this

207

negative situation. Here's an example of how you can transform a situation by changing your own responses to it. A colleague of mine was increasingly irritated by hearing her telephone ring. Whenever it rang at work, she got angry because it interrupted her work. When it rang at home in the evening, she became increasingly annoyed because it was usually an intrusive telemarketer. Eventually she realized that her constant feelings of irritation and anger were not helping the situation, and were only hurting her own well-being.

She applied the Principle of Dynamic Reversal by deciding to change how she responded when she heard the phone ring. Now, whenever the telephone rings, she uses that sound to remind her to take a deep breath, slow down, and shift into a peaceful state of mind, and she makes sure she answers the phone from this calm, peaceful place. Regardless of what the phone call is about, she's using it to do something good for herself—and by staying calm and peaceful, she is able to respond more effectively to whoever is calling her.

- **Using visualization to transform a negative situation into a positive alternative**

The process of visualization provides a way for you to apply the Principle of Dynamic Reversal in order to create a positive new reality. Research has shown that visualization—the process of creating images in our minds—is much more effective than using willpower in order to achieve a goal or bring about a change in your life.

The power of visualization to bring about transformation has been demonstrated scientifically. The key is to develop a clear vision of the goal you want to achieve—and then, in your mind, visualize yourself actually living in this new way.[38]

Visualization has the power to transform us literally—by bringing about physical changes in your own body. There are many examples demonstrating that this really happens.

A famous experiment demonstrating the power of visualization was conducted by Australian psychologist Alan Richardson.[39] He took three randomly chosen groups of students, none of whom had ever practiced visualization before, and tried three different methods of improving their basketball skills. The first group went out onto a basketball court and physically practiced making free throws every day for 20 days. The second group only practiced physically on the first and twentieth days and did nothing else. The third group physically practiced free throws only on the first and twentieth days, but in addition they visualized sinking baskets for 20 minutes every day on each of the remaining 18 days. The results? The first group, which practiced physically every day, improved 24 percent. The second group, which only practiced for two days, showed no improvement at all. But the third group, which practiced physically for two days, then engaged in visualization for 18 days, improved 23 percent—almost as much improvement as the students who had practiced physically every day! These results demonstrate the amazing power of visualization to transform us. Visualization could be described as "practicing in one's imagination."

You can use visualization to transform the negative images and beliefs about yourself that you carry in your Shadow. Believing that you are worthless or insignificant prevents you from creating the most fulfilling life for yourself. You can transform your existing mental pictures and the negative emotions associated with these thoughts, however, by replacing them with positive mental images that trigger empowering positive feelings.

Visualization allows you to actively transform yourself by reprogramming your internal imagery. When you become aware of a negative belief or negative self-image in your Shadow, think of the positive aspect you would like to hold instead. Then regularly visualize what you would feel like, and how you could act with this new positive aspect in your life. If you are getting ready to make a life transition, you can practice visualizing vivid positive images of yourself and how you want to be living in this next chapter of your life.

The key is to create clear mental images with very specific details, since extremely detailed pictures greatly strengthen the power of visualization. The more you "feel" and "see" a new positive image in your mind, the more this new mental imagery literally becomes part of you, the more it prepares you for the new reality you want to live, and the greater the results in your life.

• Transforming extreme perfectionism

For many of us, extreme perfectionism has been part of the False Self we created. Extreme perfectionism means having such high standards that they are impossible to achieve. However, because of the limited thinking styles of our False Self, we believe that if we can't be 100% perfect, all the time, every time, then we are a failure. As a result, extreme perfectionism actually prevents you from taking action for fear that you will make a mistake.

Extreme perfectionism is created by rigid beliefs about how we should be, but these beliefs limit who we are and what we can do. You can use the Principle of Dynamic Reversal to transform your enslaving beliefs and feelings that cause extreme perfectionism, so that instead you can have a more relaxed, easygoing approach to life in which you feel free to make mistakes, recognize that you can learn from your mistakes, and know that you don't have to be 100% perfect in order to be successful. Letting go of extreme perfectionism can actually help you become more effective in your work and life.

The following exercises will help you explore and apply the Principle of Dynamic Reversal.

Exercises for Principle # 6—The Principle of Dynamic Reversal:

The universe is a constant flow of ever-changing reality to which we can respond creatively.

> **Application:** You can stay centered in your True Self through both the ups and downs of life; this gives you the power to transform a negative situation, by seeing its positive potential and turning it into a positive alternative.

Exercise 6-A. Living the Principle of Dynamic Reversal: Negative aspects of my life that I've overcome or capitalized on.

Think of a negative aspect or experience in your life that you were able to overcome or capitalize on. Briefly describe what the problem was, and how you overcame or capitalized on it.

_____

_____

_____

_____

_____

_____

(If you liked this exercise, try to think of other negative aspects or experiences in your life that you overcame, and describe how you overcame or capitalized on each of them.)

Exercise 6-B. Transforming a negative aspect of your life.

Refer back to Exercise 1-B, "Positive and negative aspects of my current life" (in Chapter 3).

1. From your answers to that exercise, choose a negative aspect of your current life that you would like to transform, and write it here:

_____

_____

_____

_____

_____

2. Visualize the positive alternative that you would like to have in your life instead of this negative aspect. Write your positive vision here.

_____

_____

_____

_____

_____

_____

_____

3. Then consider how you can bring this positive alternative into your life, by creating a plan for action steps you can take in order to transform this negative into a positive alternative, and implement your plan.

_____

_____

_____

_____

_____

_____

_____

4. If you enjoyed this exercise, you can continue choosing negative aspects of your life, and work on transforming each one into a positive alternative.

_____

_____

_____

_____

_____

_____

_____

_____

Exercise 6-C. Reinforcing your vision of the New You.

To reinforce your new mental images:

1. Cut out magazine pictures that show in detail the new positive images of what you want to do and how you want to be, and place these pictures where you can see them every day.

2. For five minutes each day, look at these pictures and use the power of your imagination to create detailed mental images of yourself being, feeling and acting in this new way. As these new, more positive mental images become more real to you, ask yourself what practical steps you can take, to make this new you and your new life a reality.

215

Exercise 6-D. Transforming Perfectionism.

If perfectionism is a problem for you, center yourself and honestly answer the following questions. For every No answer, ask yourself:

Why am I stuck in this behavior? How can I transform this behavior?

Do I procrastinate because I am afraid that I will do something wrong? And if so, can I stop my tendency to procrastinate? Yes_____ No_____

Can I stop placing such high demands on myself? Yes_____ No_____

Can I stop feeling that I never accomplish enough? Yes_____ No_____

Can I stop getting upset at myself for making mistakes?   Yes_____ No_____

Do I feel that no matter what I accomplish, I don't measure up? And if so, can I stop feeling this way? Yes_____ No_____

Can I stop believing that I am never good enough? Yes_____ No_____

Can I stop believing that I am a failure if I fail? Yes_____ No_____

Can I stop feeling ashamed when I do not achieve my goals? Yes_____ No_____

Can I stop feeling driven? Yes_____ No_____

Can I stop believing that I always have to be productive? Yes_____ No_____

Can I stop thinking in All-or-Nothing terms? Yes_____ No_____

Can I stop expecting too much of myself? Yes_____ No_____

Can I stop having such a hard time dealing with failure? Yes_____ No_____

Can I stop always having to push myself harder? Yes_____ No_____

Can I change my feeling that if I can't do something perfectly, I won't try? Yes_____ No_____

Can I stop having extremely high standards for myself? Yes_____ No_____

Can I stop believing that if I'm not totally perfect, then I am a failure? Yes_____ No_____

Promoting neuroplastic changes in your brain:
The latest discoveries in brain science reveal that we can literally rewire our own brains by changing how we think or act. However, in order to accomplish this, you need to repeatedly practice the new thinking style or new behavior that you want to bring into your life. The following exercise will help you practice the Principle of Dynamic Reversal so it becomes a natural part of you.

Exercise 6-E. Continuing to transform negative aspects of your life.

Whenever you feel trapped by, or stuck, in a negative situation, remember that you have the power to transform it into a positive alternative.
When you encounter a negative situation that you want to change:

- Center yourself to reconnect to your True Self.

- Envision a positive alternative to the current situation.

- Develop an action plan for how you can transform this negative into a positive.

- Take the needed steps to implement your action plan.

SELF-DISCOVERY CHECKLIST: Steps toward your True Self	✓
1. The Principle of Mutuality. I can create dynamic balance in how I think, by moving beyond one-dimensional, All-or-Nothing thinking.	
• For any idea, I can create an opposite alternative to it, so I can now see two alternatives.	
• I can look for both the upsides and the downsides in each alternative.	
• As I envision myself standing in the middle between two opposite alternatives, I can hold the possibility of Both-And in my mind.	
• I can practice dynamic Both-And thinking.	
Comments:	
2. The Principle of Association. I can expand my thinking even further by using Continuum Thinking.	

SELF-DISCOVERY CHECKLIST: Steps toward your **True Self** *(continued)*	✓
• I can construct a mental continuum, and see the many "gray areas" between two opposite end points.	
• Instead of assuming that I have only two choices, I can see that there are many options and possibilities available to me.	
Comments:	
3. The Principle of Centeredness. I can connect to my original inner core through the practice of centering.	
• I can find a centering practice that feels right for me, and I can practice it regularly (for at least 20 minutes each day).	
• I can observe how my life changes with my regular practice of centering.	
Comments:	

SELF-DISCOVERY CHECKLIST: Steps toward your True Self *(continued)*	✓
4. The Principle of Wholeness. I can create wholeness for myself by recognizing, strengthening, and integrating previously devalued or ignored aspects of my life.	
• I can recognize undervalued areas of my life that I need to pay more attention to.	
• I can devote time and energy to strengthening missing areas of my life.	
• I can create even greater wholeness in my life by recognizing and transforming the contents of my Shadow.	
• I am willing to look at the faulty negative beliefs that I have about myself.	
• I am willing to acknowledge undesirable aspects of myself, and hurtful things I have done, that I tried to ignore.	
• I can change my behavior, so that in the future I will no longer act in these ways.	
Comments:	

SELF-DISCOVERY CHECKLIST: Steps toward your True Self *(continued)*	✓
5. The Principle of Love-in-Action. I can become more fully my True Self by expressing more love in my life, starting with love for myself.	
• I know that I am worthy of love.	
• I can give healthy self-love to myself.	
• I can devote more time and energy to expressing love for the people closest to me.	
Comments:	
6. The Principle of Dynamic Reversal. I know that I have the power to transform negative situations—past, present, and future.	
• If I feel stuck in a negative situation or thrown off-balance by stressful circumstances, I can remember to center myself so I reconnect to my True Self.	
• I can use all the abilities of my True Self to respond creatively to a negative situation.	
• I can transform a negative situation by using Both-And thinking.	

SELF-DISCOVERY CHECKLIST: Steps toward your True Self *(continued)*	✓
• I can expand my perceptions of a negative situation by reframing it, so I can discover its positive potentials.	
• I can examine my reactions to a negative situation, and I can transform my own reactions so I create more positive outcomes.	
• I can use visualization to create new positive alternatives to my old negative beliefs, and to picture myself living a more authentically successful and fulfilling new life.	
Comments:	

SEVEN STEPS TO CONNECT TO YOUR TRUE SELF

1. Expanding my thinking
2. Expanding my options
3. Being able to center myself
4.a. Becoming more whole by discovering and integrating missing aspects of my life
4.b. Transforming faulty negative beliefs about myself by exploring my Shadow
5. Being able to love myself fully
6. Developing my power to transform my past, present, and future
7.

*****

Chapter 10.

Living with Meaning and Purpose: The Principle of Universal Connectedness

Are you ready to learn why you are innately important? Are you ready to learn how to connect to the innate sources of meaning and purpose in your life?

Principle #7, the Principle of Universal Connectedness, helps you understand why you are innately important, and shows you how to create authentic meaning and purpose for your life.

7. The Principle of Universal Connectedness

The universe is an interconnected, ever-evolving reality, and your life is connected to the dynamic story of the universe.

Application: You are important and everything you do has an impact; you can affirm your innate importance by creating a unique purpose that guides your life, and by expressing your connections to the larger world around you.

You are important because you are uniquely you—and you are also important because your story is helping to create the larger story of the universe. You are a wonderful, valuable, lovable, powerful, unique individual, and you are innately important. You can affirm your innate importance by connecting to your True Self and living authentically.

But here's another Both-And: One aspect of becoming your True Self is recognizing that you are also interconnected with the universe, and interconnected with everything around you. This means that in addition to developing your own unique gifts and talents and creating personal fulfillment, in order to live authentically from your True Self, you also need to express your interconnectedness with the larger world around you. We find the deepest meaning in life when we feel open and connected to something larger than ourselves, rather than living only within the closed system of our personal lives.

At the age of 59, James H. was "retired" from his position as Chief Operating Officer at a high-tech firm—through no fault of his own, but as a cost-cutting measure (an action taken by many similar companies). Because he still based his identity on his work, James went to many executive search firms and did extensive networking—but none of his efforts turned up any new job offers, and he began to feel depressed, a man without a purpose. In my work with James, I focused on the Principle of Universal Connectedness, which helped him realize that he needed to connect to something larger than himself. Since he now had plenty of free time, he decided to volunteer at a local organization that worked with homeless children. This process of giving back and feeling connected to something larger than himself gave James a new sense of purpose, which helped him feel good about himself and eventually pulled him out of his depression. These positive changes even led indirectly to James obtaining two paid consulting positions, which generated new income equivalent to what he had been earning in his former corporate position.

The scientific basis for the Principle of Universal Connectedness

The latest scientific discoveries reveal that the universe is a dynamically evolving cosmos to which you are innately connected—an awareness that can provide you with a whole new source of personal empowerment.

In the Mechanistic model of the universe developed by Isaac Newton around 400 years ago, Newton envisioned the universe as a clock mechanism created by God—the ultimate watchmaker—who after His creation, retreated to let this clock-universe run by itself.[40] This Mechanistic cosmology teaches us to view the universe as an unchangeable machine, and to view ourselves as tiny meaningless specks in a dead, meaningless universe. This Mechanistic view can cause us to feel a deep sense of personal insignificance, believing that our lives are senseless and have no purpose.

A new cosmological model of the universe has recently emerged. Contemporary cosmology began in 1929, when astronomer Edwin Hubble discovered that galaxies are traveling away from each other and the universe is expanding; in other words, the universe is not static, but is still evolving and changing.[41]

Furthermore, the latest discoveries and theories about the origin and evolution of our universe demonstrate that we all share the same physical origins. This new scientific cosmology teaches that everything in the universe is connected and that you share the same atomic matter, patterns, and creative forces which created the stars, the planets, and the rest of the universe. Everything

228

about you—your need to find meaning, your intelligence, creativity, and desire to love and be loved—all reflect the nature of the cosmos of which you are a part.[42]

Most scientists today believe that the universe and everything in it came into being approximately 13.7 billion years ago with the fiery explosion of the Big Bang. The materials that constitute you and me, and everything else in the world—all of the energy, space, and time that make up our past, present, and future—all originated in that moment in time.

This new cosmological understanding of the universe expands our awareness by extending your concept of your ancestral genealogy all the way back to the fiery explosion of the Big Bang. More than a billion years after the Big Bang, the universe had cooled sufficiently that that primordial hydrogen and helium could coalesce into gas clouds and collapse into stars. Long before our planet Earth was formed, the atoms that made up its rocks and stones were adrift in space, having been born in the nuclear furnace and death throes of ancient stars.

Everything in the universe, past, present, and future, from atoms to stars to human beings, came from the explosion of that cosmic fireball. The molecules that make up your body were created from the death of stars billions upon billions of years ago. The oxygen you breathe, which provides life to every cell in your body, came from supernovas that exploded in space. The carbon that makes up your body likewise came from the death of a star. Also, 90% of what makes up your body comes from the most exotic material in the universe—stardust—which is made from the ashes of previous generations of burned-out stars. The calcium that makes up your bones, the iron in your blood and the oxygen that you breathe all came from the explosion of stars.[43]

The energy which makes your life possible comes from the hydrogen of our sun, which, like everything else in the universe, originated from that same primordial fireball. All the water that exists on Earth and the 73% of your body-weight made of water came from space. The universal law of gravity keeps your feet on the ground, and every rock and stone beneath your feet shares your origin from the beginning of time.

These new scientific discoveries mean that your True Self is deeply interconnected with the universe—a realization which can satisfy one of our deepest desires: to be connected with something larger than oneself. The fact is that everything you think, feel and do takes place in the context of the cosmos. Realizing that your life is a microcosm of the macrocosm of the universe can help you realize how significant your life really is.

Applying the Principle of Universal Connectedness in your life

What you believe about the nature of the universe and your place in it is not a trivial matter, since it has profound consequences for how you think about yourself and all aspects of your life. Your concept of the universe provides a framework that determines how you view yourself and creates a context for how you will live. The Principle of Universal Connectedness reminds us that the universe is a dynamically evolving cosmos, and that your story is part of this continually evolving story of the universe—an awareness that can provide you with a whole new source of personal empowerment and meaning.

- **You are innately important because your story is helping to create the story of the universe**

Knowing that the universe is in the process of evolving can give you a greater sense of your own personal significance. You can wake up each morning aware that because you are part of this ever-evolving universe, you continually have an opportunity to move forward in developing the potential of your personal True Self. This new cosmological perspective also helps you realize that your life is inherently significant because it is an integral part of the unfolding story of the cosmos, and what you do here and now contributes to the story of the ever-expanding universe.

The Principle of Universal Connectedness can also enhance your experience of significance through the realization that your life is connected with the oneness of the web of creation.

Each of us is unique, with our own unique gifts and unique purpose for being, but at another level we are all interconnected—connected to every other living being, and to the Earth, and to the larger cosmos beyond our own planet. If everything is interconnected, then everything you do has an impact—far beyond yourself. This perspective enhances your sense of significance by helping you understand that everything you do truly makes a difference.

• You can express your importance by creating a purpose for your life

You are important, and your life is important. Creating a sense of purpose for yourself—a purpose that comes from your True Self—is an essential aspect of affirming your innate importance.

If you are living from your False Self, you can still find a purpose to guide your life—but it will probably be an external purpose such as making the most money, getting the highest-ranking position, always being a winner. In fact, many of us are motivated by a goal or purpose that someone else has created.

A key to living authentically is to discover or create your own unique life purpose. Knowing what your authentic purpose is can give you a reason why you want to get up in the morning, and can keep you on track, so you're not distracted by getting caught up in goals or activities that are not really important or meaningful for you. Your authentic life purpose will also allow you to develop and express your many gifts and talents.

Finding an authentic purpose for yourself is especially important when you have gone through—or are getting ready to go through—a major life-transition. Since you can no longer fall back on your old role, you need a new purpose to guide you and give your life meaning. While going through a transition can be stressful, this major change in your life also gives you the opportunity to create a new purpose for yourself. Instead of having to meet someone else's needs or criteria, you can create a purpose for yourself that is guided by your own values. In fact, the latest scientific research suggests that our need to have a purpose in life may actually be innate within us, because not only can having a purpose in life bring meaning to your life; it can even keep you healthy.

A recent study published in the *Journal of the Association for Psychological Science* said that feeling you have a sense of purpose in life helps people live longer, no matter what your age.[44] A study conducted by the National Academy of Science found that purpose in life is linked with better mental and physical health.[45] Another study concluded that having higher levels of purpose in life actually reduces the deleterious effects of Alzheimer's disease![46]

A well-defined sense of purpose provides you with a reference for making successful decisions regarding what you want to do in the next chapter of your life. When I was living from my False Self, my life's purpose was narrowly defined by external goals such as striving to be a winner and earning the most money. But a key aspect of living from your True Self is discovering or defining your own unique life-purpose according to your own goals and values.

In order to know what you really want to do, you have to know who you really are. Your purpose has to be an expression of your True Self. That's another way in which discovering and living from your True Self can bring you authentic happiness and fulfillment.

- **Expressing your connectedness with something larger than yourself**

As the latest scientific discoveries have revealed, you are innately interconnected with the larger universe. In addition to developing your own unique gifts and talents and creating personal fulfillment, living authentically from your True Self also needs to include a way for you to express your interconnectedness with the larger world around you.

- **Creating loving, caring connections with the people around you**

   One of the most powerful ways in which we can express our interconnectedness is by showing love and caring for other people.

   In fact, the ability to create loving connections with other people and express our caring for them is literally innate within our own brains and nervous systems. As Chapter 8 explained, neuroscientists have now documented that we human beings are born with the innate capacity to receive love, express love, and connect to other people through love. Our brains and hormones actually change in positive healthy ways when we are able to connect lovingly to other people. Not only do we feel good when we are able to receive and share love, giving to others, helping others, and expressing our caring for other people can make you both happier and physically healthier.[47]

   Living from a more loving perspective can also be the foundation from which you can become a responsible, compassionate co-creator of our larger world. You can deepen and expand your capacity for love by creating loving interactions with other people—not only with those you know intimately, but also with fellow members of the larger local, national, and global communities in which you reside.

If it feels right to you, you can express your interconnectedness by choosing to contribute to creating a more just, peaceful, and humane society. You can use your new abilities and your new life to have a positive impact on larger economic and social problems, such as education, health care, and homelessness. You can become aware of social and economic problems in your community, accept their presence but not agree with them, and you can act creatively to help alleviate them. Expanding your sense of community allows you to participate in humanity's evolutionary process and help co-create a fair and equitable society and a better world.

My personal journey of connecting to my True Self has shown me that we can express love in every level of relationship: starting with love for yourself; moving out to share love with those closest to you, your family and friends; moving further out to express your interconnectedness with and love for people in your community, nation, and globally; and finally by expressing your interconnectedness with and love for our Earth and all its inhabitants. Since we are all interconnected, every act of love that you or I perform will reverberate far beyond the immediate recipients, spreading both openly and unrecognized through the world and helping to restore wholeness in larger, unexpected ways.

- **Expressing your connectedness through a new relationship with the Earth**

As I view myself and the world from the perspective of our interconnectedness, I become aware that my body is 90 percent water, and I am connected to all the water on this planet. We continue to pollute our rivers, lakes, oceans, and even the underground aquifers from which we get our drinking water perhaps not realizing that it takes an aquifer thousands of years to clean itself.

I could describe many other examples of how we are polluting and harming the Earth and its many inhabitants—plants, animals, and humans. Hearing such devastating statistics can be emotionally overwhelming, even paralyzing, and can make us give up in despair. This is where a more balanced perspective can give us power, hope, and guide our actions. Such a perspective can help us see that our material prosperity need not be achieved at the expense of the Earth's well-being. In our actions, we can give back to, as well as take from, the Earth.

Another fascinating branch of new scientific research suggests that our bodies and minds are innately connected with the natural world; research now shows that we need to spend time in Nature, and that being disconnected from Nature actually impairs our physical and mental well-being. Some people describe the harm caused by our disconnection from Nature as "nature deficit disorder."

This new research shows that spending time in Nature, interacting directly with the Earth and with the denizens and processes of the natural world, can boost our mental acuity and creativity; improve our physical and mental health and wellness; and can strengthen our connections with other people. For example, one well-known research study showed that hospital patients who were able to look out of their windows at trees actually healed more quickly than patients who looked out of their windows and only saw a wall. Because of findings such as this, many health care facilities and retirement communities now actively include access to green plants, trees and other forms of the natural world in their designs and activities.[48]

The following exercises will help you become more aware of both your own innate importance and your interconnectedness with the larger world around you, and will help you begin thinking about what you can do so your life feels more significant and meaningful.

Exercises for Principle #7—The Principle of Universal Connectedness:

The universe is an interconnected, ever-evolving reality, and your life is connected to the dynamic story of the universe.

Application: You are important and everything you do has an impact; you can affirm your innate importance by creating a unique purpose that guides your life, and by expressing your connections to the larger world around you.

Exercise 7-A. Experiencing your innate importance and your interconnectedness.

Think of a time when you felt genuinely important, or when your life felt truly significant. Perhaps this feeling came because you had a clear purpose in life, or you felt connected to something larger than yourself. Write about this feeling of significance, and why you felt this way.

Exercise 7-B. Strategies for developing self-confidence.

This exercise will help you develop a stronger sense of confidence in your ability to make substantive changes in your life, so you can create a truly authentic life. It incorporates the fact that "success breeds success."

1. Make a list of your past successes. This will help you feel more confident that you will be able to live from your True Self.

2. List activities you can do that will move you out of your comfort zone. These actions will help you feel more confident that you can actually do what is necessary to express your uniqueness.

Exercise 7-C. My life is important.

In the chart below, list as many reasons you can think of for why you deserve to feel that you are inherently important.

- **Read these reasons aloud to yourself, anytime you begin doubting that you are inherently important, or anytime you have a low sense of self-esteem.**

I am inherently important because:
I am inherently important because:
I am inherently important because:
I am inherently important because:
I am inherently important because:
I am inherently important because:

I am inherently important because:
I am inherently important because:
I am inherently important because:

Exercise 7-D. Making my life count.

Think about and answer the following questions:

- **What can I do so I feel that my life counts? How can I make a difference?**

_____

_____

_____

_____

_____

_____

_____

Exercise 7-E. Creating a Significance List.

A Bucket List puts in writing all the activities you want to do before you die. A Significance List is a list of all the important or truly meaningful things you want to do before you die. A Significance List helps fill your life with meaning, and as you actually implement these activities, it enables you to feel proud of your life when you look back on it later.

List all the important things you want to do before you die:

_____

_____

_____

_____

_____

_____

_____

_____

Promoting neuroplastic changes in your brain:

The latest discoveries in brain science reveal that we can literally rewire our own brains by changing how we think or act. In order to accomplish this, you need to repeatedly practice the new thinking style or new behavior that you want to bring into your life.

The following exercise will help you practice the Principle of Universal Connectedness so it becomes a natural part of you.

Exercise 7-F Creating a Vision Statement for your more authentic new life.

Reconnecting to your True Self allows you to live more authentically. You can begin now by developing a Vision Statement of a more authentic life that you would like to live. To be effective, your Vision Statement needs to have a strong emotional appeal that both captures your imagination and engages your spirit. It also needs to express what you deeply want your life to be, yet it has to be realistic enough to enable you to picture yourself actually living it.

Seven Vision Killers

The following can prevent you from creating a compelling vision of your new life:

- Not taking the time to create a vision
- Believing that you cannot create a vision for yourself
- Assuming that your life in the future will be the same
- Fear of making a mistake
- Not actually wanting your life to change

- Believing that you do not deserve a happy and fulfilling life

Guidelines for creating an inspiring vision for your life:

1. Give yourself permission to dare to dream what you previously thought was not possible, by going beyond the limitations of "should," "could" or "would."

2. Keep it simple; you should know your vision so well that you can say it any time as an elevator speech. Make it meaningful, short, sweet, and to the point, and you will not only be able to remember it, you will be able to achieve it!

3. Make it energizing and inspiring.

4. Be specific in describing how your new life will be guided by your True Self.

5. Refer to this vision regularly, to remind you of what you want your new life to be.

6. Know it, believe it, and work to make it happen in your daily life.

7. If necessary, revise it. If the current version of your vision is not working, throw it out! Do not view this as a mistake, since your life's circumstances change, and your vision may also need to change.

In the space below, describe your vision for your new, more authentic life.

In order to make it more real to you, read this vision each day.

My Vision Statement for my new, more authentic life:

Now that you've gone through all the steps of the System for Self-Discovery, here is a final checklist with which you can document your progress toward becoming your True Self.

SELF-DISCOVERY CHECKLIST: Steps toward your True Self	✓
1. The Principle of Mutuality. I can create dynamic balance in how I think, by moving beyond one-dimensional, All-or-Nothing thinking.	
• For any idea, I can create an opposite alternative to it, so I can now see two alternatives.	
• I can look for both the upsides and the downsides in each alternative.	

SELF-DISCOVERY CHECKLIST: Steps toward your True Self *(continued)*	✓
• As I envision myself standing in the middle between two opposite alternatives, I can hold the possibility of Both-And in my mind.	
• I can practice dynamic Both-And thinking.	
Comments:	
2. The Principle of Association. I can expand my thinking even further by using Continuum Thinking.	
• I can construct a mental continuum, and see the many "gray areas" between two opposite end points.	
• Instead of assuming that I have only two choices, I can see that there are many options and possibilities available to me.	
Comments:	
3. The Principle of Centeredness. I can connect to my original inner core through the practice of centering.	
• I can find a centering practice that feels right for me, and I can practice it regularly (for at least 20 minutes each day).	

SELF-DISCOVERY CHECKLIST: Steps toward your True Self *(continued)*	✓
• I can observe how my life changes with my regular practice of centering.	
Comments:	
4. The Principle of Wholeness. I can create wholeness for myself by recognizing, strengthening, and integrating previously devalued or ignored aspects of my life.	
• I can recognize undervalued areas of my life that I need to pay more attention to.	
• I can devote time and energy to strengthening missing areas of my life.	
• I can create even greater wholeness in my life by recognizing and transforming the contents of my Shadow.	
• I am willing to look at the faulty negative beliefs that I have about myself.	
• I am willing to acknowledge undesirable aspects of myself, and hurtful things I have done, that I tried to ignore.	
• I am willing to forgive myself for these aspects and activities.	

SELF-DISCOVERY CHECKLIST: Steps toward your True Self *(continued)*	✓
• I can change my behavior, so that in the future I will no longer act in these ways.	
Comments:	
5. The Principle of Love-in-Action. I can become more fully my True Self by expressing more love in my life, starting with love for myself.	
• I know that I am worthy of love.	
• I can give healthy self-love to myself.	
• I can devote more time and energy to expressing love for the people closest to me.	
Comments:	
6. The Principle of Dynamic Reversal. I know that I have the power to transform negative situations—past, present, and future.	

SELF-DISCOVERY CHECKLIST: Steps toward your True Self *(continued)*	✓
• If I feel stuck in a negative situation or thrown off-balance by stressful circumstances, I can remember to center myself so I reconnect to my True Self.	
• I can use all the abilities of my True Self to respond creatively to a negative situation.	
• I can transform a negative situation by using Both-And thinking.	
• I can expand my perceptions of a negative situation by reframing it, so I can discover its positive potentials.	
• I can examine my reactions to a negative situation, and I can transform my own reactions so I create more positive outcomes.	
• I can use visualization to create new positive alternatives to my old negative beliefs, and to picture myself living a more authentically successful and fulfilling new life.	
Comments:	

SELF-DISCOVERY CHECKLIST: Steps toward your True Self *(continued)*	✓
7. The Principle of Universal Connectedness. I can become more fully my True Self by recognizing that I am innately important, and by expressing my interconnectedness with the world around me.	
• I know that I am innately important.	
• I know that my life is contributing to the larger story of the universe.	
• I know that everything I do has an impact, and makes a difference in the world.	
• I can find meaning in my life by connecting to something larger than myself.	
• I can discover or create a purpose for my life.	
Comments:	

SEVEN STEPS TO CONNECT TO YOUR TRUE SELF

1. Expanding my thinking

2. Expanding my options

3. Being able to center myself

4.a. Becoming more whole by discovering and integrating missing aspects of my life

4.b. Transforming faulty negative beliefs about myself by exploring my Shadow

5. Being able to love myself fully

6. Developing my power to transform my past, present, and Future

7. Expressing both my own unique purpose and my interconnectedness with the larger world around me

*****

Chapter 11.

Creating an Authentic Life for Yourself: Next Steps

Now that you've read through this book and worked on the Exercises, you've begun the process of discovering and connecting to your True Self.

You probably expereinced new feelings and emotions as you went through this process of self-discovery. You may have felt emotions of fear, confusion, surprise—and you may also have felt the satisfaction, even exhilaration of breaking free, leaving the cocoon of your False Self and flying high as you experienced what it means to be your True Self.

This is just the beginning. You've spent many years living from the habitual identity of your False Self, and now you're working on breaking free from your old beliefs, emotions, and reactions. It will take time—and repeated practice—so that your True Self can fully emerge.

It takes time to change, to break all those old False-Self habits and transform your old False-Self beliefs, which were built from many different intellectual, emotional, and psychological habits.

To fully bring your True Self into the world:

- You need to keep on changing intellectually. You need to keep on developing and integrating the new balanced way of thinking about who you really are, about how the world works, and about your role in the world.

- You need to keep on changing psychologically. You need to continue recognizing false negative beliefs that you hold about yourself; continue being aware of their triggers; and continue creating new, more genuine positive alternatives to these negative beliefs.

- You need to keep on changing emotionally. You need to be aware of your feelings of fear and shame; keep reminding yourself that you are more than these limiting emotions; and you need to recognize how, the more you connect to your True Self, the more supportive emotions of healthy pride, love, satisfaction, and joy come into your life.

As you continue to explore your True Self and keep practicing these new beliefs and acting differently, you will feel yourself changing. You will begin to look at the world differently. You may want to do things differently, and you may even change how you relate to the people in your life. You may realize that there are new goals you now want to accomplish.

In other words, the more you become your True Self, the more you will find yourself wanting to shift out of your old way of living and create an authentic new life for yourself. **The more you connect to your True Self, the more you will want to redesign your life so it allows you to express your newly-discovered True Self.**

You can create a more authentic life no matter where you are in your life-story. If you are getting ready to make a major transition in your life—such as leaving your current full-time work—you now have an especially good opportunity to consciously and purposefully create the next chapter of your life, based on the goals, values, and passions of your True Self.

It's also essential for you to remember that going through a major life-transition (such as a mid-life crisis, divorce, loss of a loved one, becoming an empty-nester, leaving your full-time work, changing careers, life threatening medical issues, letting go of your business, or retiring) can cause significant stress in your life, and stress can throw you back into the old ways of your False Self. It's especially important

257

for you to have a firm sense of who you truly are—to stay connected to your True Self—when any of these life-transitions happens in your life.

Creating a plan for an authentic new life guided by your True Self

Up until now, you have been creating your life based on the conscious and unconscious beliefs, emotions, and habits of your old False Self. It takes time to make your life congruent with who you really are. You don't want to accidentally fall back into your False-Self ways of thinking, feeling, or acting. Having begun the process of connecting to your True Self, you want to continue deepening and strengthening this connection. This means that you now need to create a new life that supports your emerging True Self, and keeps on bringing you the freedom to be who you really are.

Three types of support are essential as you develop your True Self and move into a new, more authentic life.

1. You need to create a structured, comprehensive written plan for your future, based on the new goals, abilities, and passions of your True Self. Many studies have shown that having a written plan for your future is essential for achieving that future. In order to live as a whole person, your

plan also needs to be comprehensive. You need to examine each area of your life (for example, as depicted in the "Pie-Chart" in Exercise 4-C), so you can develop a plan for how you will more fully express your True Self in each of these areas.

2. <u>In order to create a structured, comprehensive plan for a more authentic new life, you also need to develop a clear purpose for your life guided by who you truly are.</u> Having a clear purpose for your life gives you the motivation, enthusiasm, and energy for creating your authentic new life.

3. <u>You need to find sources of social and emotional support to help you keep going with your self-transformation process.</u> Sources of social and emotional support might come from your spouse or a close friend (or any combination of these). You might also want to connect to other people who are going through their own process of authentic self-discovery.

If you have an upcoming transition, it's especially important that you think about and plan your new life based on who you really are. Without a plan for your post-transition life, you may feel a loss of enthusiasm for life, become bored or depressed, feel that there is nothing to look forward to, or feel that your life no longer has meaning or purpose. Lack of a carefully thought-out plan for one's future can cause people to make poor life decisions and rash choices, in the false hope that they can make sense out of life once more.

Even if you are not going through a specific transition, as you continue to connect to your True Self, you will eventually realize that now it's time for you to create a new plan for your life—a plan that comes from the goals and values of your True Self and is congruent with the genuine purpose of your life.

Creating a purposeful plan for your life gives you the opportunity to re-examine what you are currently doing, so you can decide if it is an expression of your old False Self. This also allows you to consider other goals and activities, that can reinforce your connection to your True Self. A structured, comprehensive written plan for your more authentic new future serves as a launching pad from which the butterfly of your True Self can fly high, allowing you to experience new awareness, new energy, and new enthusiasm for your life.

You may have a trusted advisor with whom you can work in order to develop a comprehensive,

purposeful written plan for your authentic future life.
The Successful Transition Planning Institute and our
colleagues around the world also offer many
resources that can guide and support you as you go
through the continuing process of connecting to your
True Self and creating a more authentic new life. (See
Chapter 12.)

*****

Chapter 12.

Resources to Help You Live More Authentically in the Next Chapter of Your Life

This book provides the launching pad for you to begin your transformational journey to living a life of transcendence.

Self-actualization is not at the top of Maslow's hierarchy of needs, self-transcendence is. Maslow saw a number of problems with having self-actualization at the apex of his motivation needs, so he created a new sixth level - that of self-transcendence, which satisfies one of our deepest needs to be connected to something larger than ourselves. Maslow did not have time to make this additional top level on his hierarchy of needs well known, since he died of a heart attack shortly after his realization.

- **Self-Transcendence: Living at the Top of Maslow's Hierarchy of Needs workshop**

In these four weekly one hour on-line sessions with Jack Beauregard and a group of fellow participants, you will connect further to your True Self through an in-depth, non-traditional, non-dogmatic spiritually-oriented exploration that helps you reach "Self-Transcendence"—the top of Maslow's Hierarchy of Needs. The sessions help you rise to a higher spiritual level within yourself, expand the way you think and how you view yourself so you can connect with the oneness of creation. The on-line presentations provide time for Q&A, and the program includes follow-up workbooks, so you can continue the process of spiritual self-exploration and self-development on your own in between sessions.

- **Self-Actualization: My New Life ™ online workshop**

In these eight weekly one hour on-line sessions with Jack Beauregard and a group of fellow participants, you go in-depth to transform yourself emotionally, intellectually and psychologically so you can live to your fullest potential, be the person that you were meant to be and live a successful and fulfilling life of significance. In the self-actualization workshop you will apply the power of authenticity, the deep spiritual nature of your True Self, and your higher connection to the transcendence level to transform the way you think and feel about yourself.

- **Creating a Purposeful Life of Authenticity ™ Self-Directed Handbook/online workshop program**

In this program you will apply the corresponding strategic steps of the 7 principles of authenticity to express your True Self in your daily life. You will also learn how you can create a purposeful life by applying a step-by-step methodology to choose meaningful activities in all ten aspects of your life which resonate with your True Self.

Visit see **www.The PlatinumYears.com** For more information to help you continue on your journey of self-discovery and support you in creating an authentic new life for yourself.

- **Speaking Engagements by Jack Beauregard**

Jack Beauregard, STPI's founder and CEO, has many years of experience as a workshop presenter, guest speaker, and conference keynote presenter. For more information, or to invite Jack to your organization or conference, contact him at:

jack@theplatinumyears.com
800.414.9405

Programs offered by the Successful Transition Planning Institute

Here are brief descriptions of related programs and resources offered by the Successful Transition Planning Institute (STPI):

- ### Self-Assessment Programs:

The programs in this category are designed to encourage your own self-reflection. Each of the following programs includes an on-line Questionnaire that you fill out, a personally-customized Report that analyzes your responses, and a Workbook you then use to follow up on the recommendations in your Report.

- ### — Exploring Your Life, Shaping Your Future ™

This self-assessment program for professionals and corporate executives helps you achieve clarity around leaving your current full-time work and creating an authentic new future for yourself. It includes an on-line Questionnaire, a personally-customized Report analyzing your responses, and a follow-up Workbook to encourage your further self-reflection.

— **What's Next? Self-Assessment** ™
(For business owners)

This self-assessment program for business owners helps you get clarity around transitioning your company to new owners and moving on to a fulfilling new future. It includes an on-line Questionnaire, a personally-customized Report analyzing your responses, a copy of our highly-acclaimed book *Finding Your New Owner: For Your Business, For Your Life* by Jack Beauregard, and a companion Workbook to encourage your further self-reflection.

- **Short-term Coaching Programs:**

In each of the following programs, you work one-on-one with an STPI-certified Transition Advisor or Transition Planning Consultant (in person or via computer), using structured discussion and client Workbooks.

— **Explore Coaching Program for Late-Career Executives and Professionals** ™

This short-term coaching program for late-career executives and professionals provides structured discussion, advice, and client Workbooks to help you gain clarity around transitioning out of your current full-time work and creating a fulfilling new future for yourself.

— What's Next? Coaching Program for Baby Boomer Business Owners ™

Using structured discussion, accountability, client Workbooks and Jack Beauregard's highly acclaimed book *Finding Your New Owner: For Your Business, For Your Life*, this short-term coaching program for Baby-Boomer business owners helps you gain clarity around transitioning your company to new owners and creating a fulfilling new future for yourself.

— Living with Purpose Workshop ™

A one- or two-day workshop presented by an STPI-certified Transition Planning Consultant, for professionals, executives, and business owners who are planning to leave their current position, to help you think about and plan a fulfilling new life for yourself. The workshop includes presentations, handouts, and discussion. (For information about Workshops currently being offered, or to request a Workshop in your area, contact Jack@theplatinumyears.com

- **In-depth Coaching Program:**

Living with Purpose One-to-One coaching

In this eight-week program, you work one-on-one with an STPI-certified Transition Planning Consultant (either in person or online), expanding your thinking to help you get in touch with what you really want to do in the next chapter of your life, so you can create a comprehensive plan for a new life you can't wait to live. This program includes: taking an in-depth look at 10 different areas of your life, doing a System Analysis, making Final Decisions and developing Tactical Implementation Plans for creating a new life. It also includes an analysis of your unique Decision-Making Style, your personally customized Decision-Making Style Report, and a Final Report presenting the complete plan that you developed for your future. (This program also includes input from your spouse or life-partner.)

- **Personal Transition Planning Training**

If you would like to learn about training to become a Transition Planning Consultant or a Transition Advisor, contact the Successful Transition Planning Institute at info@theplatinumyears.com

NOTES

1. The Mechanistic Paradigm: see Edward Harrison, *Masks of the Universe* (N.Y.: MacMillan Publishing Company, 1985).

2. Some examples of the new cosmology include Carl Sagan, *Cosmos* (N.Y.: Random House, 1980); Edward R. Harrison, *Cosmology: The Science of the Universe* (N.Y.: Cambridge University Press, 1981); John D. Barrow and Joseph Silk, *The Left Hand of Creation: The Origin and Evolution of the Expanding Universe* (N.Y.: Oxford University Press, 1983); Paul Davies, *The Cosmic Blueprint: New Discoveries in Nature's Creative Ability to Order the Universe* (New York/London: Simon & Schuster, 1992); and Lisa Randall, *Dark Matter and the Dinosaurs: The Astounding Interconnectedness of the Universe* (N.Y.: HarperCollins, 2015).

3. We live in an ever-evolving universe: see John D. Barrow and Joseph Silk, *The Left Hand of Creation: The Origin and Evolution of the Expanding Universe* (N.Y.: Oxford University Press, 1983). Each of us is personally connected to the dynamic forces and creative patterns of the universe: see Fritjof Capra, *The Tao of Physics* (N.Y.: Bantam New Age, 1984). How we think influences the reality we experience: see Norman Cousins, *Head First: The Biology of Hope* (N.Y.: Dutton, 1989). By changing how we think and act, we can literally "re-wire" our own brains: see Norman Doidge, M.D., *The Brain that Changes Itself: Stories of Personal Triumph from the Frontiers of Brain Science* (N.Y.: Penguin Books, 2007).

4. Your beliefs create your reality: see Maxwell Maltz, M.D., *Psycho-Cybernetics* (N.Y.: Pocket Books, 1971); Norman Cousins, *The Healing Heart: Antidotes to Panic and Helplessness* (N.Y.: W. W. Norton & Co., Inc., 1983); Norman Cousins, *Head First: The Biology of Hope* (N.Y.: Dutton, 1989); Bill Moyers, *Healing and the Mind* (N.Y.: Doubleday, 1993); Deepak Chopra, M.D. and Rudolph E. Tanzi, Ph.D, *Super Brain: Unleashing the Explosive Power of your Mind to Maximize Health, Happiness, and Spiritual Well-Being,* (N.Y.: Harmony Books/Random House, 2012); and article on "Mind-body medicine," from the University of Maryland Medical Center, www.umm.edu/Health/Medical/AltMed/Treatment/Mindbody-medicine

5. The incident at the Monterey Park football stadium: Norman Cousins, *The Healing Heart: Antidotes to Panic and Helplessness* (N.Y.: W. W. Norton & Co., Inc., 1983), pp. 205-206; see also "'Hysteria' among possible causes of illness of 125 at game on coast," http://www.nytimes.com/1982/10/24/us/hysteria.

6. The experiment with the medical students was described in Barry Blackwell, Saul S. Bloomfield, and C. Ralph Buncher, "Demonstration to Medical Students of Placebo Responses and Non-Drug Factors," *The Lancet*, Vol. 299, No. 7763, 10 June 1972, pp. 1279-1282.

7. Jack Beauregard saw a video of this experiment with the pike in a training workshop several years ago.

8. Edward Harrison, *Masks of the Universe* (N.Y.: MacMillan Publishing Company, 1985).

9. We live in a dynamic, continually changing universe characterized by numerous coherent systems, with new order arising out of chaos: See for example Erich Jantsch, *The Self-Organizing Universe* (N.Y.: Grove Press, Inc., 1974); Erich Jantsch, *Design for Evolution: Self-Organizing and Planning in Life and Human Systems* (N.Y.: G. Braziller, 1975); John D. Barrow and Joseph Silk, *The Left Hand of Creation: The Origin and Evolution of the Expanding Universe* (N.Y.: Oxford University Press, 1983); John Briggs and David Peat, *The Turbulent Mirror: An Illustrated Guide to Chaos Theory and the Science of Wholeness* (N.Y.: Harper & Row, 1989); Paul Davies, *The Cosmic Blueprint: New Discoveries in Nature's Creative Ability to Order the Universe* (New York/London: Simon & Schuster, 1992); Fritjof Capra, *The Web of Life* (N.Y.: Doubleday, 1996); and James Gleick, *Chaos* (N.Y.: Viking, 1998).

10. "Did You Know: The Regeneration Speeds of the Human Body," www.feelguide.com, November 13, 2010.

11. On neuroplasticity: Sharon Begley, *Train Your Mind, Change Your Brain: How a New Science Reveals our Extraordinary Potential to Transform Ourselves*, (N.Y.: Ballantine Books/Random House, 2007); and Norman Doidge, M.D., *The Brain that Changes Itself: Stories of Personal Triumph from the Frontiers of Brain Science* (N.Y.: Penguin Books, 2007).

12. "Did You Know: The Regeneration Speeds of the Human Body," www.feelguide.com, November 13, 2010.

13. Your beliefs create your reality: See for example Maxwell Maltz, M.D., *Psycho-Cybernetics* (N.Y.: Pocket

Books, 1971); Norman Cousins, *The Healing Heart: Antidotes to Panic and Helplessness* (N.Y.: W. W. Norton & Co., Inc., 1983); Norman Cousins, *Head First: The Biology of Hope* (N.Y.: Dutton, 1989); Bill Moyers, *Healing and the Mind* (N.Y.: Doubleday, 1993); Deepak Chopra, M.D. and Rudolph E. Tanzi, Ph.D, *Super Brain: Unleashing the Explosive Power of your Mind to Maximize Health, Happiness, and Spiritual Well-Being,* (N.Y.: Harmony Books/Random House, 2012); and article on "Mind-body medicine," from the University of Maryland Medical Center, www.umm.edu/Health/Medical/AltMed/Treatment/Mindbody-medicine For additional examples of how our mental images can shape our experiences, also see notes 38 and 39 below, on "Visualization."

14. For more about neuroplasticity and how, by changing how you think and act, you can literally "rewire" your own brain and improve your life, see Daniel G. Amen, M.D., *Change Your Brain, Change Your Life* (N.Y.: Three Rivers Press, 1998); Sharon Begley, *Train Your Mind, Change Your Brain: How a New Science Reveals our Extraordinary Potential to Transform Ourselves,* (N.Y.: Ballantine Books/Random House, 2007); Norman Doidge, M.D., *The Brain that Changes Itself: Stories of Personal Triumph from the Frontiers of Brain Science* (N.Y.: Penguin Books, 2007); Daniel J. Siegel, M.D., *Mindsight: The New Science of Personal Transformation* (N.Y.: Bantam Books, 2011); Teresa Aubele, PhD, et al., *Train Your Brain to Get Happy: The Simple Program that Primes your Gray Cells for Joy, Optimism, and Serenity* (Avon, MA: Adams Media/F+W Media, 2011); Marsha Lucas, PhD, *Rewire your Brain for Love: Creating Vibrant Relationships Using the Science of Mindfulness* (Carlsbad, CA: Hay House, 2012); and Deepak Chopra, M.D. and Rudolph E. Tanzi, Ph.D, *Super Brain: Unleashing the*

Explosive Power of your Mind to Maximize Health, Happiness, and Spiritual Well-Being, (N.Y.: Harmony Books/Random House, 2012.)

15. "How Long Does It Actually Take to Form a New Habit? (Backed by Science)," www.huffingtonpost.com, April 10, 2014.)

16. The universe is shaped by relationships of dynamic balance: Menas Kafatos and Robert Nadeau, *The Conscious Universe* (N.Y.: Springer-Verlag, 1994). Kafatos and Nadeau say that "in modern physics…virtually every major advance in physical theories describing the structure and evolution of the universe has been accomplished by the emergence of new complementarities" (p. 127), and "Complementarity is the fundamental structuring principle in our conscious constructions of reality" (p. 128).

17. Malcolm W. Browne, (1990-08-21), "New Direction in Physics: Back in Time," *The New York Times,* Retrieved 2010-05-22. http://www.nytimes.com/1990/08/21/science/new-direction-in-physics-back-in-time.html?pagewanted=all

18. The Big Bang: See Carl Sagan, *Cosmos* (N.Y.: Random House, 1980); or Edward R. Harrison, *Cosmology: The Science of the Universe* (N.Y.: Cambridge University Press, 1981).

19. On matter and antimatter: Guinevere Kauffmann, "Thermal history of the Universe and early growth of density fluctuations (PDF), Max Planck Institute for Astrophysics. Retrieved 2016-01-

06; J. Beringer et al. (Particle Data Group), "Big-Bang cosmology" *Phys. Rev.* D86, 010001 (2012): (21.43); "The discovery of geomagnetically trapped cosmic ray antiprotons," – *Astrophysical Journal Letters* - .*http://arxiv.org/pdf/1107.4882v1.pdf*; and "Integral Discovers the Galaxy's Antimatter Cloud is Lopsided" - http://www.esa.int/Our_Activities/Space_Science/I ntegral/Integral_discovers_the_galaxy_s_antimatter_ cloud_is_lopsided

20. Dynamic balance in our cells: "Osmosis, Water Channels, and the Regulation of Cell Volume", Section 15.8, *Molecular Cell Biology. 4th edition* - http://www.ncbi.nlm.nih.gov/books/NBK21739/

21. Balance between populations of owls and mice: "Trophic Links: Predation and Parasitism", University of Michigan, Global Change - http://www.globalchange.umich.edu/globalchange1/ current/lectures/predation/predation.html

22. Roger L. Martin, *The Opposable Mind: How Successful Leaders Win Through Integrative Thinking* (Boston, MA: Harvard Business School Press, 2007.)

23. On Lukasiewicz's many-valued logic system, see entry for "Jan Lukasiewicz" in the *Stanford Encyclopedia of Philosophy*: www.plato.stanford.edu/entries/lukasiewicz

24. On "fuzzy logic," see Bart Kosko and Satoru Iska, "Fuzzy Logic," *Scientific American*, July 1993, p. 80; also Daniel McNeill and Paul Freiberger, *Fuzzy Logic* (N.Y.: Simon & Schuster, 1993).

25. On the physical, mental, emotional, and behavioral impacts of meditation, see for example Sharon Begley, *Train Your Mind, Change Your Brain: How a New Science Reveals our Extraordinary Potential to Transform Ourselves* (N.Y.: Ballantine Books/Random House, 2007); Teresa Aubele, PhD, et al., *Train Your Brain to Get Happy: The Simple Program that Primes your Gray Cells for Joy, Optimism, and Serenity* (Avon, MA: Adams Media/F+W Media, 2011); Tim Ryan, *A Mindful Nation: How a Simple Practice Can Help Us Reduce Stress, Improve Performance, and Recapture the American Dream* (Carlsbad, CA: Hay House, 2012); Marsha Lucas, PhD, *Rewire your Brain for Love: Creating Vibrant Relationships Using the Science of Mindfulness* (Carlsbad, CA: Hay House, 2012); and Gretchen Reynolds, "How Meditation Changes the Brain and Body," *New York Times/on-line*, February 18, 2016.

26. Norwich U. using meditation: https://www.bostonglobe.com/news/nation/2012/1 2/01/meditation-study-seeks-help-cadets-prevent-ptsd/w5tntwkaJXRPsZjFJrNPEK/story/html

27. U.S. military using meditation: http://www.nydailynews.com/life-style/health/u-s-marines-learn-meditate-stress-reduction-program-article-1.1245698; and http://psychcentral.com/news/2013/03/03/military-may-be-turning-to-meditation-for-ptsd/52149.html

28. On holarchies and wholeness in the universe and in our lives, see Fritjof Capra, *The Turning Point* (N.Y.: Bantam, 1982); David Bohm, *Wholeness and the Implicate Order* (Boston, MA: Ark Paperbacks, 1983); and John Briggs and David Peat, *The Turbulent Mirror: An Illustrated Guide to Chaos Theory and the Science of Wholeness* (N.Y.: Harper & Row, 1989).

29. On the functions of the two sides of the brain, see Susan Gall, *The Gale Encyclopedia of Psychology* (Detroit, MI: Gale Research, 1996), articles on "Left-Brain Hemisphere," pp. 224-225 and "Right-Brain Hemisphere," pp. 311-312.

30. See article on "Corpus Callosum" in www.biology.about.com

31. On integrating reason and emotions, see Antonio R. Damasio, "The Emotional Brain," *Scientific American,* June 1997.

32. On the "Shadow," see Carl C. Jung, *Man and His Symbols* (N.Y.: Dell Publishing, 1964).

33. Our unconscious beliefs, memories, etc. have a powerful impact on our lives: see Susan Gall, *The Gale Encyclopedia of Psychology* (Detroit, MI: Gale Research, 1996), article on "Repression," p. 309.

34. For more about Toxic Shame, see Andrew P. Morrison, M.D., *Culture of Shame* (N.Y.: Ballantine Books, 1996); and John Bradshaw, *Healing the Shame that Binds You* (Deerfield Beach, FL: Health Communications, 2005).

35. For more about the physiological and neurological bases of human connection, and the physical and emotional benefits of participating in loving relationships and engaging in loving actions, see Alan Luks with Peggy Payne, *The Healing Power of Doing Good: The Health and Spiritual Benefits of Helping Others* (Lincoln, Nebraska: iUniverse.com, Inc., 1991); Stephen Post, Ph.D. and Jill Neimark, *Why Good Things Happen to Good People: How to Live a Longer,*

Healthier, Happier Life by the Simple Act of Giving (N.Y.: Broadway Books, 2007); Susan Kuchinskas, *The Chemistry of Connection: How the Oxytocin Response Can Help You Find Trust, Intimacy, and Love* (Oakland, CA: New Harbinger Publications, 2009); Marsha Lucas, PhD, *Rewire your Brain for Love: Creating Vibrant Relationships Using the Science of Mindfulness* (Carlsbad, CA: Hay House, 2012); and Amy Banks, M.D. with Leigh Ann Hirschman, *Four Ways to Click: Rewire your Brain for Stronger, More Rewarding Relationships* (N.Y.: Jeremy P. Tarcher/Penguin, 2015.)

36. The history of the universe is a history of constant transformation: Carl Sagan, *Cosmos* (N.Y.: Random House, 1980); Edward R. Harrison, *Cosmology: The Science of the Universe* (N.Y.: Cambridge University Press, 1981); John D. Barrow and Joseph Silk, *The Left Hand of Creation: The Origin and Evolution of the Expanding Universe* (N.Y.: Oxford University Press, 1983); and Michael S. Turner, "The Origin of the Universe," *Scientific American*, September 2009.

37. Change is stressful, and stress shifts us into more limited ways of thinking and acting: Robert M. Sapolsky, *Why Zebras Don't Get Ulcers: A Guide to Stress, Stress-Related Diseases, and Coping* (N.Y.: W.H. Freeman, 1998); Kimberley V. Oxington, *The Psychology of Stress* (Hauppauge, NY: Nova Science Publishers, 2005).

38. Using visualization to change yourself and your experiences: Maxwell Maltz, M.D., *Psycho-Cybernetics* (N.Y.: Pocket Books, 1971); Shakti Gawain, *Creative Visualization: Use the Power of Your Imagination to Create What You Want in Your Life* (N.Y.: New World Library, 2002); Robin Nixon, *Creative Visualization for Dummies* (Hoboken, NJ: John Wiley, 2011); article

about "Guided Imagery" on "WebMD,"
www.webmd.com/balance/stress.management/tc/gu
ided-imagery-topic-overview; and article about
"Sports Visualization" at
www.sportsmedicine.about.com

39. Alan Richardson's basketball and visualization
experiment:
https://goalop.wordpress.com/2012/06/13/visualiz
e-your-sports/

40. The Mechanistic Paradigm: Edward Harrison,
Masks of the Universe (N.Y.: MacMillan Publishing
Company, 1985).

41. The universe is still evolving and changing: Carl
Sagan, *Cosmos* (N.Y.: Random House, 1980); Edward
R. Harrison, *Cosmology: The Science of the Universe* (N.Y.:
Cambridge University Press, 1981); John D. Barrow
and Joseph Silk, *The Left Hand of Creation: The Origin
and Evolution of the Expanding Universe* (N.Y.: Oxford
University Press, 1983).

42. We are made of the same stuff and same patterns
as the universe: Erich Jantsch, *The Self-Organizing
Universe* (N.Y.: Grove Press, Inc., 1974); Erich
Jantsch, *Design for Evolution: Self-Organizing and
Planning in Life and Human Systems* (N.Y.: G. Braziller,
1975); Carl Sagan, *Cosmos* (N.Y.: Random House,
1980); Edward R. Harrison, *Cosmology: The Science of
the Universe* (N.Y.: Cambridge University Press, 1981);
Fritjof Capra, *The Tao of Physics* (N.Y.: Bantam New
Age, 1984); Menas Kafatos and Robert Nadeau, *The
Conscious Universe* (N.Y.: Springer-Verlag, 1994); Lisa
Randall, *Dark Matter and the Dinosaurs: The Astounding
Interconnectedness of the Universe* (N.Y.: HarperCollins,
2015).

43. We are made of the same stuff as the stars: Burbridge, Burbridge, Fowler, and Hoyle, "Synthesis of the Elements in Stars," *Reviews of Modern Physics*, 1957.

44. *Journal of the Association for Psychological Science* article on purpose and longevity: http://www.npr.org/sections/health-shots/2014/07/28/334447274/people-who-feel-they-have-a-purpose-in-life-live-longer.

45. National Academy of Science study says that having a life purpose is linked to better physical and mental health: http://www.pnas.org/content/111/46/16331.abstract

46. Having a life purpose can reduce the impact of Alzheimers: http://www.ncbi.nlm.nih.gov/pmc/articles/PMC3389510/

47. For more about the physical, emotional, and other benefits of engaging in loving actions, see Alan Luks with Peggy Payne, *The Healing Power of Doing Good: The Health and Spiritual Benefits of Helping Others* (Lincoln, Nebraska: iUniverse.com, Inc., 1991); Stephen Post, Ph.D. and Jill Neimark, *Why Good Things Happen to Good People: How to Live a Longer, Healthier, Happier Life by the Simple Act of Giving* (N.Y.: Broadway Books, 2007.); and Emma Seppala, Ph.D., *The Happiness Track: How to Apply the Science of Happiness to Accelerate your Success* (N.Y.: HarperCollins, 2016).

48. For more about our innate need to connect to the natural world, see Richard Louv, *The Nature Principle: Reconnecting with Life in a Virtual Age* (Chapel Hill, NC: Algonquin Books/Workman Publishing, 2011); Eva M. Selhub, M.D. and Alan C. Logan, *Your Brain on Nature: The Science of Nature's Influence on Your Health, Happiness, and Vitality* (N.Y.: HarperCollins, 2014); and Florence Williams, "This is Your Brain on Nature: When we get closer to nature—be it wilderness or a backyard tree—we do our overstressed brains a favor," *National Geographic* magazine on-line, January 2016; ngm.nationalgeographic.com/featurehub

ABOUT THE AUTHOR

After founding a successful medical supply company that he built into a multi-million dollar business, Jack Beauregard founded Innervisions Associates, an organizational transformation firm that has helped business, health, and educational leaders expand their thinking to open up new possibilities for themselves and their organizations. Jack is now the CEO of the Successful Transition Planning Institute, which he founded to teach his unique methodology to help business owners, professionals, and corporate executives connect to their authentic selves so they can create successful and fulfilling new lives. STPI has now become an internationally recognized thought-leader in personal and business transition planning, with STPI-certified associates on four continents. Through Innervisions Associates and STPI, Jack has helped thousands of people examine and reframe their lives so they can become more self-aware and more authentically successful and fulfilled. Jack is also a popular speaker who has presented his unique approach nationally and internationally, on radio, television, and as a conference keynote speaker.

For more information about STPI's resources and programs for professionals, executives, business owners, and advisors, see

www.ThePlatinumYears.com